BrightRED Study Guide

CfE HIGHER

MEDIA

Wendy Elrick and Keith Hay

First published in 2020 by:
Bright Red Publishing Ltd
1 Torphichen Street
Edinburgh
EH3 8HX

Copyright © Bright Red Publishing Ltd 2020.

Cover image © Caleb Rutherford

All rights reserved. No part of this publication may be reproduced, stored in a retrieval system, or transmitted in any form or by any means, electronic, mechanical, photocopying, recording or otherwise, without prior permission in writing from the publisher.

The rights of Wendy Elrick and Keith Hay to be identified as the authors of this work have been asserted by them in accordance with sections 77 and 78 of the Copyright, Designs and Patents Act 1988.

A CIP record for this book is available from the British Library

ISBN 978-1-84948-308-7

With thanks to:
PDQ Digital Media Solutions Ltd (layout), Laura Booth (copy-edit) and Clodagh Burke (proof-read)

Cover design and series book design by Caleb Rutherford – eidetic

Acknowledgements

Every effort has been made to seek all copyright holders. If any have been overlooked, then Bright Red Publishing will be delighted to make the necessary arrangements.

Permission has been sought from all relevant copyright holders and Bright Red Publishing are grateful for the use of the following:

Thamizhpparithi Maari/Creative Commons (CC BY-SA 3.0)[1] (p 7); Lars Plougmann/Creative Commons (CC BY-SA 2.0)[2] (p 7); Roge/Creative Commons (CC BY-SA 2.0)[2] (p 8); Carlo Alfredo Clerici/Creative Commons (CC BY 2.0)[3] (p 8); tugol/Shutterstock.com (p 10); Stefano Buttafoco/Shutterstock.com (p 10); Audrius Merfeldas/Shutterstock.com (p 10); Michael/Creative Commons (CC BY 2.0)[3] (p 11); GNOME Project /Creative Commons (CC BY-SA 3.0)[1] (p 11); Sixflashphoto/Creative Commons (CC BY-SA 4.0)[4] (p 11); Dcubillas/Creative Commons (CC BY-SA 3.0)[1] (p 11); Life of Riley/Creative Commons (CC BY-SA 4.0)[4] (p 11); Boris Thaser/Creative Commons (CC BY 2.0)[3] (p 11); Monkey Business Images/Shutterstock.com (p 14); mary981/Shutterstock.com (p 15); Jemastock/Shutterstock.com (p 15); Marco Verch/Creative Commons (CC BY 2.0)[3] (p 15); Bogyofunk/Shutterstock.com (p 16); indra-east/Shutterstock.com (p 16); Faiz Zaki/Shutterstock.com (p 16); WheelieMonkey/Shutterstock.com (p 17); Thea van Duin/Creative Commons (CC BY-ND 2.0)[5] (p 18); Nicholas LabyrinthX/Creative Commons (CC BY-SA 2.0)[2] (p 18); Prayitno/Creative Commons (CC BY 2.0)[3] (p 19); DocChewbacca/Creative Commons (CC BY-SA 2.0)[2] (p 20); Logo reproduced by permission of WWF (p 20); Irina Gheorghita/Creative Commons (CC BY 2.0)[3] (p 21); Bert Kaufmann/Creative Commons (CC BY-SA 2.0)[2] (p 21); Thomas T./Creative Commons (CC BY-SA 2.0)[2] (p 22); Dean Drobot/Shutterstock.com (p 22); Piotr Zajda/Shutterstock.com (p 22); Sueby Sue/Shutterstock.com (p 22); 4045/Shutterstock.com (p 22); GettysGirl4260/Creative Commons (CC BY-SA 2.0)[2] (p 22); Danomyte/Shutterstock.com (p 23); Blan-k/Shutterstock.com (p 23); Monkey Business Images/Shutterstock.com (p 23); JD Hancock/Creative Commons (CC BY 2.0)[3] (p 23); Volha Shaukavets/Shutterstock.com (p 24); Boston Public Library/Creative Commons (CC BY 2.0)[3] (p 26); dun_deagh/Creative Commons (CC BY-SA 2.0)[2] (p 26); Karen Eliot/Creative Commons (CC BY-SA 2.0)[2] (p 26); 3Dstock/Shutterstock.com (p 26); LiliGraphie/Shutterstock.com (p 28); Images Money/Creative Commons (CC BY 2.0)[3] (p 31); rnl/Shutterstock.com (p 31); littlenySTOCK/Shutterstock.com (p 34); Martin Coles/Creative Commons (CC BY-ND 2.0)[5] (p 34); GraphicsRF/Shutterstock.com (p 36); Raph_PH/Creative Commons (CC BY 2.0)[3] (p 37); Anton Balazh/Shutterstock.com (p 37); alex lang/Creative Commons (CC BY-SA 2.0)[2] (p 38); Marcus Ward/Creative Commons (CC BY-ND 2.0)[5] (p 38); sergio barbieri/Creative Commons (CC BY-SA 2.0)[2] (p 39); William Warby/Creative Commons (CC BY 2.0)[3] (p 40); Marian Galovic/Shutterstock.com (p 41); E Greens/Creative Commons (CC BY 2.0)[3] (p 41); HstrongART/Shutterstock.com (p 46); PlusONE/Shutterstock.com (p 47); zef art/Shutterstock.com (p 47); Hans Splinter/Creative Commons (CC BY-ND 2.0)[5] (p 49); Vilkas Vision/Shutterstock.com (p 50); fyv6561/Shutterstock.com (p 50); Pat Bianculli/Creative Commons (CC BY-ND 2.0)[5] (p 51); Derek Keats/Creative Commons (CC BY 2.0)[3] (p 52); qvist/Shutterstock.com (p 53); Ian McKellar/Creative Commons (CC BY-SA 2.0)[2] (p 54); Abi Skipp/Creative Commons (CC BY 2.0)[3] (p 54); Two photos by Everett Historical/Shutterstock.com (p 54); sirtravelalot/Shutterstock.com (p 55); Nick Webb/Creative Commons (CC BY 2.0)[3] (p 64); Woody Hibbard/Creative Commons (CC BY 2.0)[3] (p 64); Pietro Zanarini/Creative Commons (CC BY 2.0)[3] (p 68); Mark Poprocki/Shutterstock.com (p 69); kosmos111/Shutterstock.com (p 69); Lindebornt/Creative Commons (CC BY-ND 2.0)[5] (p 69); Malgorzata Litkowska/Shutterstock.com (p 70); clivewa/Shutterstock.com (p 71); Bernard Goldbach/Creative Commons (CC BY 2.0)[3] (p 73); Josh Hallett/Creative Commons (CC BY-SA 2.0)[2] (p 74); Tiago Cassol Schvarstzhaupt/Creative Commons (CC BY 2.0)[3] (p 76); David Shankbone/Creative Commons (CC BY 2.0)[3] (p 78); UN International Criminal Tribunal for the former Yugoslavia/Creative Commons (CC BY 2.0)[3] (p 79); Oxy_gen/Shutterstock.com (p 81); Andrey_Popov/Shutterstock.com (p 81); Robert Scoble/Creative Commons (CC BY 2.0)[3] (p 82); Rawpixel.com/Shutterstock.com (p 83); David Michalczuk/Creative Commons (CC BY 2.0)[3] (p 84).

[1] (CC BY-SA 3.0) https://creativecommons.org/licenses/by-sa/3.0/
[2] (CC BY-SA 2.0) http://creativecommons.org/licenses/by-sa/2.0/
[3] (CC BY 2.0) http://creativecommons.org/licenses/by/2.0/
[4] (CC BY-SA 4.0) https://creativecommons.org/licenses/by-sa/4.0/
[5] (CC BY-ND 2.0) http://creativecommons.org/licenses/by-nd/2.0/

Printed and bound in the UK.

INTRODUCTION

Introducing Higher Media 4

ANALYSIS

Language

Introducing analysis and camera shots 6

Camera angles and editing 8

Lighting and colour 10

Sound 12

Mise en scène 14

Print media 16

Representation

People, creatures, places 18

Ideas and events 20

Narrative

Narrative structures 1 22

Narrative structures 2 24

Narrative codes 1 26

Narrative codes 2 28

Categories

Genre and purpose 30

Form, medium, style, tone and more 32

Audience

Audience demographics/Mode of address 34

Readings of a text 36

Institution

Internal constraints 38

External constraints 40

ASSESSMENT

External assessment 1 42

External assessment 2 44

External assessment 3 46

ROLE OF THE MEDIA

Overview 48

Meeting audience needs 50

Meeting purposes of institutions 52

Influencing behaviour 54

Assessment 56

Assessment Example 58

PRODUCTION

Production 60

Audience and research 62

Institution research 64

Content research 66

Planning 68

Location scouting, technology and copyright 70

PRODUCTION ROLES

Recording production 72

The director 74

The camera operator 76

The editor 78

The producer 80

Radio 82

The web designer 84

THE ASSESSMENT

Evaluation 86

Unit assessment 88

The assignment – planning 90

The assignment – development 92

GLOSSARY 94

INTRODUCTION

INTRODUCING HIGHER MEDIA

THE PURPOSE OF THIS BOOK

This guide has one priority: to help you achieve. By picking this up, you've already shown that you are committed to success!

Media is a creative subject that brings together a whole range of skills from lots of different curriculum areas. Whether you are studying it for the first time or have progressed through other qualifications, Media allows you to engage with the real world around you in a way that is meaningful and practical. You both examine professional content and take on the role of a producer to create your own.

KEY ASPECTS

Much of the analysis and evaluation of content concerns seven key areas. These are known as the key aspects. They are:

Categories	These could include form, medium, **genre**, style, tone or purpose. Categories refers to the ways that media content is sorted into different types.
Narrative	Here you will use codes, **conventions** and theories to analyse story. You will also see how these affect the audience that consumes them.
Language	In this area, you will examine the meaning of such elements as use of camera, **mise en scène**, sound, editing, **fonts** and so forth. This matters both when looking at existing content and when thinking about making your own.
Representation	Representation is broadly how people, places and events are depicted. It also helps you examine the underlying message or ideas held by the producers.
Audience	Here you look at audience targeting and audience readings (mainly preferred, negotiated, differential and oppositional). You may also learn about demographic groups.
Institution	This involves examining who owns and controls media content, as well as looking at what **constraints**, both internal and external, producers face.
Society	Society is to do with the historical time and cultural **context** of the production of the content (Note: not covered in book but see Digital Zone for more information).

The course aims to give learners:

- the ability to analyse and create media content, appropriate to purpose, audience and context
- knowledge and understanding of the key aspects of media literacy
- knowledge and understanding of the role of media within society
- the ability to plan and research when creating media content, as appropriate to purpose, audience and context
- the ability to self-evaluate.

There are two optional units in Higher Media: *Analysing Media Content* and *Creating Media Content*.

ONLINE

Go to our Digital Zone to find out more about society.

ANALYSING MEDIA CONTENT

This unit focuses on examining existing media content and building up your analysing skills. At Higher level, you are expected to do this in a detailed and complex way. You will analyse the internal key aspects of media content using categories, narrative, representation and language and the external context of audience, institution and society. You will also examine how the internal aspects are affected by the external ones.

contd

Another important part of analysis is exploring the role of the media. This is focused on how media content meets needs, influences behaviour and **attitudes** and achieves purposes. You will also be introduced to some of the debates concerning the media.

CREATING MEDIA CONTENT

During the *Creating Media Content* unit, you are responsible for making some kind of media content. It is where you draw in your production skills and breaks down into three main areas: planning and research, making, and evaluating. You will need to work with others, so this also helps build your team-working skills. It is likely that you will also engage with technology to create your product. The key aspects are useful to help you think up and organise your ideas and also to help evaluate how well you have created your content and the impact it has.

There is also the externally assessed exam.

EXTERNAL EXAM

The external exam is divided into three parts. There are two question papers and an assignment. The total amount of available marks is 130.

Question papers

These are the exams sat during the exam diet in May under exam conditions. It consists of two papers: Paper One (Analysis of Media Content) is focused on analysing content and context, while Paper Two is The Role of Media.

The Analysis of Media Content paper is worth 50 marks and the Role of the Media paper is worth 20.

Analysis of Media Content is divided into two sections. There are two questions focused on media content and context that ask you to apply the key aspects to texts you have studied in class. Each question is worth 20 marks. The second section asks you to analyse and compare two unseen texts (from a choice of film posters, magazine covers or print adverts). This is worth 10 marks. You will have two hours and 30 minutes to complete this question paper.

The Role of the Media paper has one question worth 20 marks. You will have one hour to complete this paper.

Paper 1	2 questions – you answer both	Analysis of content and context	2 × 20 marks
	1 question – you select option a, b or c	Unseen textual analysis	10 marks
Paper 2	1 question	Role of Media	20 marks

Assignment

The assignment involves you planning, researching, making and evaluating media content on your own. You will be set a brief by your teacher and the assignment will be completed by a deadline to allow it to be assessed by the SQA externally. You will be assessed on your content as well as your research and planning choices and your final evaluation of your product. There are 60 marks available for this section of the exam.

ONLINE

Go to our Digital Zone to access links to example question papers.

THINGS TO DO AND THINK ABOUT

There are many different areas that your teacher can choose to explore with you as well as a lot of possibilities when making your content. You should reflect on your learning and aim to link the knowledge gained in the two units together.

The 'Things to do and think about' section in every chapter contains useful suggestions for you to try. There may be activities to help you develop your analysis or production skills. They can be used as an introduction to some of the areas you need to examine as well, consolidation of your knowledge or as revision of what you have learned.

Analysis
LANGUAGE

INTRODUCING ANALYSIS AND CAMERA SHOTS

AN INTRODUCTION TO ANALYSIS

Initially, the key aspects will appear to be separate and discrete. However, the more that you practise analysing media texts, the more you will see that they are all interconnected and integrated with one another.

A media text has been carefully crafted, using narrative, representation, technical and **cultural codes** (known as *language*), and particular categories. These aspects of *content* not only interact with one another, but are set within one (or more than one) *context*. A media text is created or **encoded** by an institution using these aspects of content. The text is encoded with a particular audience in mind. That audience lives within a society, and they will *decode* the text accordingly. These three contexts interact and influence the manner in which a text is received, which will, in turn, influence the creation of new texts.

In this first chapter, Language will be explained. This involves technical codes – where meaning is created by the mechanical apparatus used to create the text, and cultural codes – which are a system of signs whose meaning is shared by members of a particular culture. There is some overlap here with the cultural codes organised by French scholar Barthes, which will be dealt with in a later chapter.

Like English, media uses the idea of **denotation** and **connotation**. The denotation (or literal meaning) of a **shot** may be to allow the audience to see everything surrounding the main character or setting. However, the connotation (which deals with the suggested, often emotional meaning) may be that the character is utterly isolated, or that they have found peace. It is these connotations that the makers of media texts are looking to use to manipulate the message.

VIDEO LINK

Head to www.brightredbooks.net/subjects to watch *The Miller and the Sweep*.

CAMERA SHOTS

Cinema's early days were only able to be recorded from a single camera, fixed on a tripod. It gives the impression of being at the theatre and watching a play. *The Miller and the Sweep* was filmed in 1897, right at the start of cinema's history.

As technology improved, the imagination of film makers began to explore different shots and angles.

Each type of camera shot is used for different reasons.

Close up

An extreme close-up would be used to focus on a character's eyes or mouth and allows the audience to see a reaction (often emotional) clearly. When used with an object, it highlights the object's importance within the text at that moment.

The close-up usually shows the character's head and shoulders. This is used to clarify dialogue and show the emotion behind the dialogue through facial expression. When used of an object, it will highlight the importance of that object to the text as a whole.

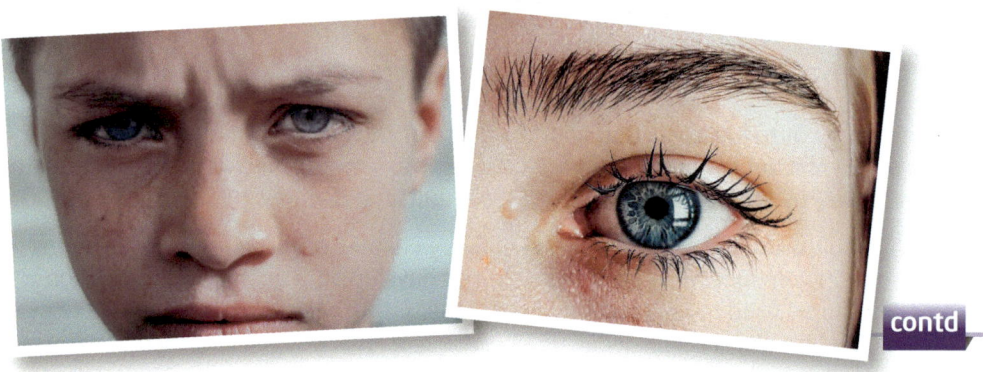

contd

Analysis: Introducing analysis and camera shots

Medium shot

A medium shot will show a human from the waist up and will be used to show action and allow for dialogue to be heard clearly. Medium shots of objects show how the object is being used within the text.

Long shot and master shot

As the camera moves backward, a long shot shows a whole human figure and is used primarily for action (think sports coverage). It can also show a bit of background, although that role is more often fulfilled by an extreme long shot (also known as a wide shot). Both the long shot and the extreme long shot, when used of objects or places, are establishing shots. They establish, in the audience mind, the place or the context for the action.

During the filming of a text, this long shot, that keeps all the players and scene in shot, is called the **master shot**. It will record the entire scene from start to finish, from the long-shot distance.

Wide shot

One particular type of wide shot is the bird's-eye shot, where the camera is flown over the subject as a bird would fly. This will have the effect of showing the audience a wide area or of showing the subject in the context of an environment (a ship on an ocean, perhaps).

OTHER TYPES OF SHOT

Where the camera takes the place of a subject in a direct manner, a point-of-view shot is created. This adds an element of immediacy for the audience as they are now totally immersed in the action, and is often used in horror films.

These shots are understood to refer to having only one subject on screen. A Two Shot (or Three Shot) will involve having two subjects (or three) in shot at the same time. This can be used to show the emotional reactions to words and actions without having to cut away, creating a more immediate and life-like conversation.

Camera shots are designed to allow the audience to understand the text more easily. With that in mind insert shots can bring the audience's attention to important actions or props. For instance, where we see a security guard leaving a building (in long or medium shot) there may be an insert shot added in close-up showing him locking the door, before the master shot returns to him walking away in long shot. The insert highlights the locking action to the audience.

DON'T FORGET

A shot is not a take. A take is an attempt to capture the action on film, using a particular shot. There may be several takes/attempts to get the action in the shot correct.

THINGS TO DO AND THINK ABOUT

Think of a film you have watched recently. Can you remember and identify the types of shots used and think of why those shots were taken? Next time you are set to watch a film, try to notice the shot types being used as you go and whether they are effective (or ineffective!).

ANALYSIS

CAMERA ANGLES AND EDITING

CAMERA ANGLES

Cameras have come a long way since *The Miller and the Sweep*. Not only can they turn to film at different angles, but they are also portable and can follow the action and the actors wherever they go. There are a number of **camera angles** and movements that are key:

- **High angle** – when the camera looks down on the subject, making it seem small, insignificant or vulnerable.
- **Low angle** – when the camera looks up at the subject, making it seem big, powerful and highly important.
- **Dutch angle** (or **Dutch tilt**) – when the camera is placed at an angle (equivalent of the audience tilting their heads to one side). The horizon appears at an angle and it is often used to show psychological or physiological illness in the subject.
- **Pan** – where the camera moves slowly across from side to side (on a fixed axis – it doesn't go up or down).
- **Tilt** – where the camera moves up and down on a fixed axis (it doesn't go left or right).
- **Crane** – where the camera is mounted on a crane and can move around at distance from the ground.
- **Tracking** – where the camera follows the action, moving alongside the subject (used often in sports, especially last 100 m of a race).
- **Rolling** – the camera tracking but diagonally (often used to show that a character is drugged or ill).

EDITING

Editing is a term that is used to describe the process of looking at all the footage that has been shot during the filmmaking process and placing it into the desired order.

There are two areas to concentrate on: *duration* (how long does each shot last?) and *transition* (how is each shot joined to the next?)

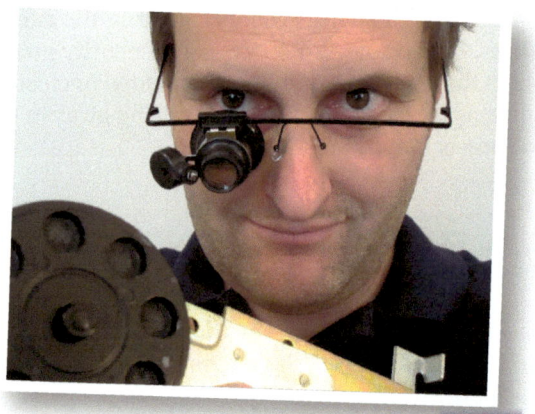

contd

Duration

Shots are like sentences in written English. A long sentence will be full of description, but will slow the action down. Short sentences speed action up. They have no description. They can create tension. On the other hand, a longer sentence will diffuse the tension by allowing the reader time to get used to events.

A short shot duration can create action and tension. Holding a shot longer will allow the audience a chance to relax and discover what is going on.

Transition

When a film has been created on film stock then the editor must literally *cut* the film and stick it together with another piece. When it has been created digitally then this process is handled by computers.

An editor has various methods of splicing (sticking together) two pieces of film – digitally or manually.

- **Straight cut** – the most normal. One scene is replaced by another. A good editor will manage to do this so that the audience aren't aware it's happening. It will appear natural.
- **Fade-out** (fade-to-black) – would suggest an ending to a section or the film.
- **Fade-in** – would suggest the opening of a scene or section of the film.
- **Dissolve** – where one image is brought in slowly while the other **fades**.
- **Wipe cut** – one image wipes across the screen to replace the other.
- **Jump cut** – a sudden change from one image to another.
- **Graphic match** (match cut) – where an incoming image is matched with the previous one in some manner.

Sequence shot

A particular shot that could incorporate different shots and angles, and that removes the need to create transitions between shots, is a *sequence shot*.

This is where a single, long take moves through different locations either through a camera mounted on a dolly (rails or multi-directional) or through the use of a **Steadicam**.

Examples of this can be seen in *Atonement* (2007), which allows the audience to immerse themselves in the chaos of Dunkirk beach before the evacuation of the British troops in May/June 1940.

THINGS TO DO AND THINK ABOUT

1. Go back and re-watch *The Miller and the Sweep*. On paper, plan out which camera angles and shots you would use if you were to re-film it today, using a single digital camera and portable tripod.

2. Write down all the connotations that come to your mind when you think of the Scottish Highlands. Now, watch the Scottish Highlands Tourist Advert at www.brightredbooks.net/subjects

   a. Count the number of edits/cuts there are in this advert (that's each time the shot changes – a new scene or a different angle for the current one).

   b. Write down all the activities shown in the advert.

   c. What do you think Visit Scotland are suggesting about the Highlands by using such editing techniques?

 VIDEO LINK

Watch a video of the portrayal of the evacuation of Dunkirk beach in *Atonement* on www.brightredbooks.net/subjects

 VIDEO LINK

Watch an extract from *Spectre* at www.brightredbooks.net/subjects which gives the audience access to James Bond's mind, showing how things are interconnected and how they slip easily from one thing to another in order to get the mission done.

 **DON'T FORGET**

A media text needs to tell a story or convey a message. Should the audience not be able to interpret or read the message or story correctly, then the production has failed. Through the use of language codes, the correct message can be held in place (**anchored**) for the audience. The camera represents the audience's viewpoint. By changing how the camera sees things, the audience's viewpoint can be changed also.

 ONLINE TEST

Test your knowledge of camera shots and angles at www.brightredbooks.net/subjects

ANALYSIS
LIGHTING AND COLOUR

LIGHTING

Lighting helps to convey the mood or atmosphere of the screen being observed.

The audience's attention can be guided by brightly lighting an object or gesture, while keeping other, minor areas, in relative darkness. At the same time, a director can use shadows to build suspense by hiding elements (or characters) from the audience.

Even something as simple as a news interview will be lit to make sure that the audience get the right message.

The most common form of lighting is three-point lighting, which uses a back light, fill light and key light. Changing the relative strength of these lights allows for different **effects** to be created – or for the subject to be well lit.

The back light, situated behind the subject, is used to highlight the subject away from the background, making them easier to see when they move.

The key light, situated in front and (usually) to the subject's right, creates the detail of the subject's image. **High key** lighting is used where the subject needs to be seen clearly (in fashion shoots, for example). Low key lighting can be used to create mood, as with the example (left) – where the back light has been removed also. See how the subject blends into the background?

The problem with the key light is that it creates shadow on the subject, since it is only coming in from one side. Hence the fill light, which comes in from the other side, and removes the shadowing.

The example below shows the effect of a key light (left), and the addition of the fill light (right).

VIDEO LINK

Check out the clip at www.brightredbooks.net/subjects on how to use three-point lighting.

In order to change moods, the lighting needs to change. When the lighting is changed and *under lighting* is used (when the main source of light is underneath the subject) then characters or objects will appear distorted. It is often used in horror films.

A similar, moody effect can be created with top lighting (where the main source of light is above the character or object). However, glamour photography also uses top lighting.

When the main source of light moves to behind the character or the object, then silhouette is created. This blocks the face of a character or detail of an object from the

contd

Analysis: Lighting and colour

audience and so can be a negative effect, or can focus on the light source or the shapes formed in the silhouette, which can be positive.

A particular technique that is used both in film and still photography called 'catch lighting' can allow an audience to identify with a character, or not. The catch light is a highlight in the eye of the subject that provides depth and a life-like spark to the subject. In turn, this allows the audience to be more sympathetic towards them as emotions and thoughts can be more easily decoded. Equally, antagonists may have the catchlight deliberately removed, to deaden their eyes.

In the example (right), the happiness of the girl has been highlighted by the catchlight.

The catch light effect is used in a more intense manner in anime, where extreme close-up shots of the character are often used to highlight emotional reactions.

COLOUR

Colour works on the audiences subconscious mind to create a mood. Soap powder boxes are more often blue than yellow as research has shown that people feel that blue will have a gentler cleansing action than yellow.

Each colour has its own connotations, which can be influenced by culture, conventions or **beliefs**. For instance, the colour red connotes a wide range of things in the North-Western Hemisphere. Love, anger and danger are all part of what red can mean.

However, in the Far East, red is a colour for good luck, which is why, for Chinese New Year, there is such a predominance of red in the decorations.

Colour can also be discussed in terms of saturation. This means that brightness and depth of the colour. A film in technicolour, for example the colour portions of *The Wizard of Oz*, are very bright and colourful. This would be described as highly saturated and carries connotations of a happy, upbeat atmosphere. It may also suggest a certain unnaturalness to the setting. In contrast, unsaturated colour, where the scene seems washed out and grey, can be used to create a sense of grittiness and harsh reality. This is frequently a feature of films that are categorised as British Social Realism such as *The Angel's Share*.

THINGS TO DO AND THINK ABOUT

1. Create a page of your own photographs that show the use of light as mentioned above. You should have at least three photos – back, over and under.

   In each case, annotate the photo, highlighting: what light source was used; which mood or atmosphere has been created; and how an audience would be expected to react to the image.

2. Copy the diagram below into your notes and for the colours – red, orange, yellow, green, blue, purple, brown and pink – note down the connotations that each colour suggests.
   You can discuss this with others to see if the connotations are the same.

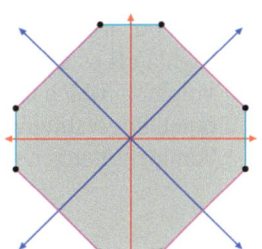

DON'T FORGET

In order to engage an audience with a media text, the producers will hope to use emotions. When watching a film, lighting and colours all guide the audience to particular emotional responses.

ONLINE TEST

Test your knowledge of lighting and colour at www.brightredbooks.net/subjects.

11

ANALYSIS

SOUND

THE ADDITION OF SOUND

In the early days of silent movies, a live piano or organ was used to accompany the images on the screen. In 1927, *The Jazz Singer* was released as the first feature-length film with fully recorded sound.

Like colour, adding sound was a huge investment for the film companies – but the technology proved to be so effective and exciting for audiences that soon all films became 'talkies'.

Now, the soundtrack is a highly digitised combination of dialogue, music and sound effects.

There are, basically speaking, two kinds of sound in the world of film, **diegetic sound** and **non-diegetic sound**.

Diegetic sound

This is sound that is part of the film world that the audience is watching. This can be dialogue, music, sound effects (doorbells, cars and so on) that come from a source within the film world. It can be off screen (a kettle boiling in a kitchen) or on screen (jukebox or car radio). The aim behind diegetic sound is to help create the *diegesis* or real world of the moving image. For all that diegetic sound belongs to the world of the film, it does not necessarily need to be recorded as the film is being shot. Sound mixing and sound effects are often added in post-production.

Non-diegetic sound

Non-diegetic sound is sound that is not recognised as being part of the film world. This can be voice-over or background music. Often this is used to create a particular mood or tone. Music, particularly, is used very effectively to suggest the emotional mood of the images on the screen.

Ways of using diegetic and non-diegetic sound

These can be used in a variety of different ways, including:

Sound bridges – where a sound from one scene will continue into the next scene and helps to maintain the continuity of the film as it allows for a smoother transition between shots/scenes.

Contrapuntal or Parallel sound – sometimes, the sound (especially background music) complements the images on screen (happy sounds when there are images of children playing, for instance). This is parallel sound. When the sound does not fit with the images, then it is called contrapuntal sound.

Film scores

No film would be released today without a complex film score – a complete musical score to cover every part of the action. Directors will use music to create mood and atmosphere, which will let the audience interpret the film's events more easily.

This is achieved through:
- Pace – slow music creates tension or empathy, while fast-paced music is the cue for action (think back to the music used for the Visit Scotland advert you looked at in the section on editing; its pace dictates how the audience will react to the Highlands as a subject).
- Volume – which can create a mood of sympathy, sadness or threat when the music is quiet. Interestingly, when the volume is turned up, the threat level can be increased to imminent danger, while it may also convey triumph.

contd

- Style – whether the music playing is instrumental, popular, classical or rock can influence the way in which the audience react. A serious scene with contrapuntal opera music (such as appeared in the first *Trainspotting* film, when Ewan McGregor's character is talking through giving up heroin while the music is from *Carmen*) can make the scene less intense and add humour.
- Timbre – which describes the richness of the sound (and is sometimes called tone colour). A flute may be described as having a round, clear timbre, while an oboe is nasal and pointed. Clearly, suggesting an emotion through sound colour can be key to a scene. In horror films, a violin piece may have a piercing, eerie timbre, while in a more romantic scene the same instrument can produce something more rounded and flowing.
- Type of Instrument – brass is loud and triumphant, strings can be creepy or flowing, drums create a beat (and tension follows).

Diegetic and non-diegetic, although most often used in reference to music and sound is not exclusively used for that purpose. Non-diegetic text on screen can be used to show where and when the scene is set (for example, London, 1945), or add extra information, often for a humorous purpose. During a scene in *Trainspotting* (1996), Ewan McGregor's character has to go to a toilet in a betting shop. The word 'TOILET' is written on the door – diegetically – but the words 'The worst' and 'in Scotland' are added non-diegetically on either side to add humour.

Leitmotif

Within a film score, the composer will have used leitmotif – a phrase within the main theme that represents something or someone within the text.

During the Star Wars (Original) Trilogy, Darth Vader, Luke Skywalker and Princess Leia all have leitmotifs attached to them. The music introduces them, or their imminent arrival, to the audience. During *Casino Royale* (2006) Daniel Craig's James Bond is only 'given' his full theme, with iconic guitar riff, at the very end of the film. The composer of the score, David Arnold, did not want to use the iconic theme too early as the film shows Bond learning his trade and becoming the character everyone knows.

As a result, throughout the film, there are leitmotif moments for Bond, where the theme is hinted at in the score, but never fully revealed. Powerful brass notes can connote tension (as with John Williams's *The Imperial March (Darth Vader's Theme)*) and the audience will react accordingly.

DON'T FORGET

Sound is often used to engage the audience and **anchor** the meaning of the text. The type of music is often related to the type of feeling the text is aiming to rouse in the audience.

THINGS TO DO AND THINK ABOUT

1. Listen to a range of film music. You can often find this on radio stations such as Classic FM or Scala or online. Try and work out what techniques the composer has used such as pace, volume, style, timbre and type of instrument. Then identify what emotion the composer is trying to arouse.

2. Watch a sequence without any sound. Predict what sounds you would expect to hear. Watch it again with the sound on. Did the maker make the choices you made? If they didn't, why were they different and what was the impact?

3. Try watching a sequence and play different pieces of music over the top. What impact does this have on the scene you are seeing? How does it change the feeling of the sequence?

ANALYSIS

MISE EN SCÈNE

OVERVIEW

Mise en scène translates as 'what is put into the scene or frame' and is used to describe the setting and props; costume, hair and make-up; facial expression and body language; lighting and colour; and the positioning of characters and objects within the frame that is seen on the screen by the audience.

These are the cues that an audience will take in order to make sense of a scene.

Look at the scene above, showing a meeting of people around a table.
- The clothing of the people around the table (formal/professional) suggests that this is a business meeting of some kind.
- This is supported through the use of 'office' equipment like laptop computers, pens and paper, and the lack of other things on the table (such as food and drinks).
- The room in which the meeting is taking place is bare of anything other than the functional furniture needed for this meeting. This is not a home or informal environment. There is nothing here to suggest that there is enjoyment or relaxation in this room.
- The woman at the far end of the table is the leader of this meeting. She is standing, which places her physically over the others and her body language suggests that she is speaking, while the body language of the others suggests they are paying attention to her.
- The lighting is bright – this is set during the day, which is further support for the business meeting reading.

Consciously or not, the audience will use semiotics (the study of signs and symbols) to help them interpret what is happening in a scene or sequence. Audiences will also recognise **icons**.

BREAKING DOWN THE MISE EN SCÈNE

Setting

Film makers spend large amounts of pre-production time in choosing the right locations and settings.

Setting can be used to manipulate an audience by building (or removing) expectations. A horror movie set in a modern/contemporary setting may be more effective than a gothic-style mansion (because it does not fit the expectations based on genre conventions).

Props

Props (short for properties) is the name given to objects that are in the set.

contd

Analysis: Mise en scène

Usually, it refers to objects that will play a part in the action (like a bottle of poison) rather than objects in the background that are used to create the set.

Costume

Costume plays an important role in mise en scène because it can instantly show the audience the personality, social status and career of a character. Costume tells the audience the particular time period concerned and which part of society within that time. Specific genres may require specific costumes.

Make-up

In early cinema, make-up was used to highlight features of the actors' faces as the film quality was not able to pick out detail very well. In modern cinema, especially with the use of IMAX, this is no longer the issue and make-up artistry has, on the whole, come to specialise in two areas: 1) making it look like no one has make-up on – so that characters look as natural as possible and 2) 'prosthetic' make-up – wounds, bruises and 'gore'.

Facial expressions/body language

Acting on stage means that the physical distance the audience is from the action limits the effectiveness of actors' expressions, unless they are exaggerated and accompanied by hand gestures.

In film acting, however, because the camera can be in extreme close-up, the facial expressions of an actor can be used far more effectively – in keeping with normal conversation, where we are constantly being given small cues as to how the other person is feeling (or responding).

Body language

The body language of an actor can give a clear indication to the audience of social status, emotional state, thoughts and feelings. Some films require realistic body language; other films (like musicals) require something more stylised.

Positioning of characters and objects

There are various ways in which the film maker can position objects and characters within the frame.
- In the foreground – we as the audience should accept this as an important character or object, while activity or objects in the background should be less important.
- A moving body or object on a stationary background will immediately call attention to itself.
- Even spacing across a frame balances the shot; crowding to one side unbalances the shot.
- Physical positioning of characters to show mood – arguing people will be at distance (physical distance reflects the emotional distance).

 ONLINE

The clip on our Digital Zone shows that mise en scène is not just important in the creative industries, but needs to be considered any time a video is being produced. Watch it and check off what is being said against what you have learned in this chapter.

DON'T FORGET

Posters, theatre productions, films, adverts, television shows; in all cases the mise en scène has to be taken into consideration.

 ONLINE TEST

Test your knowledge of lighting, colour and sound at www.brightredbooks.net/subjects.

THINGS TO DO AND THINK ABOUT

Think it, Do it.

You are a filmmaker with a basic set: a room with a window and a bed. There are two actors. Turn it into a scene from a horror film by adding whatever you wish in terms of props and costumes and by placing the actors (including facial expressions). You may choose colours and lighting.

Draw the scene and write a description of what you have created, explaining each choice along the way: colours, positions, props, costumes and so on.

Once you have done that, re-do the exercise but for a) a science-fiction film and then b) a children's fairy tale.

ANALYSIS
PRINT MEDIA

ONLINE

There are plenty of websites and other areas to look at; however, a fair beginners' guide can be found at www.brightredbooks.net/subjects

FONTS AND TYPOGRAPHY

When any media text is being created, a great deal of thought goes into the choosing and setting of the typography – the font and the wording. Just as particular colours or body language could convey a message, so the font carries connotations of the institution using it.

Fonts come *serif* or *sans serif*, where serif refers to the little 'flick' at the ends of a letter. *Arial* is a ready example of a sans-serif font. The letters are straight, without adornment. Sans-serif fonts are seen as friendly, open, boring or plain and are preferred by people who have difficulty in reading. On the other hand, serif fonts can be seen as old-fashioned, stately, reliable or historic.

Certain media texts have a very distinctive or set style. These have been thought through and created over a period of time. For instance, there is an accepted typography for comics/graphic novels. These are sans-serif fonts and are chosen for their ease of reading and clarity when capitalised.

Newspapers have particular fonts, too. *The Times* of London created a new standard font in 1931 – *Times New Roman*. This is a serif font, and was chosen by *The Times* to focus on the stately and reliable aspects, giving the readers the idea that the newspaper could be trusted. Ironically, in the 80 years since the font was created, the font can be read as representing something that is boring and uninspired.

Fonts relate to representation of the text and, by extension, the creating institution. Fonts are chosen for their perceived qualities to the audience (and are tested through small groups). Insurance companies will seek a font that the test groups feel embodies solidity, history and safety; engineering firms will look for something that is suggestive of flair and innovation.

Fonts for film posters are as carefully chosen as for any other text.

In the first example here, the company name would be written in a clear, sans-serif font. The letters are well spaced (the spacing is called *tracking*). The clarity of the font and the space taken up by the word is suggestive of time and space – the luxury of the title. There are no garish flashes involved in this company; what you get is what you get.

The second example is creating a completely different mood. The circle outside of the wording is clearly indicating a plate – this is an advert/logo for a restaurant. The cursive font is curved, giving a soft feel to the logo; no one likes to eat spiky things. The serif on the initial 'L' is complicated and gives the idea that time has to be spent just saying it. The food of this company is not rushed, but is something to be enjoyed.

For some **brands**, like the Harry Potter films, the font has become part of the brand image or the trademark. With Coca-Cola, for instance, the italic font can be recognised even when it is in a radically different language (something you can check for yourself using your favourite web browser).

LAYOUT/ORGANISATION

The rule of thirds

Many pieces of art (including photos and posters) can be divided into three sections. In photography, this is called the Rule of Thirds. It can be applied to still media texts also.

Look at this poster for *The Greatest Showman*.

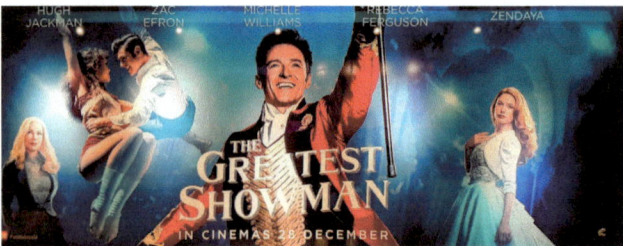

contd

By placing two vertical lines on this image, three clear sections can be seen. The first starts on the left and includes the first three characters. The second shows only the middle character, while the third is the character on the right.

The central third – focusing on the character in the red jacket – is where the audience eye is drawn initially. This is the largest character, and so we can assume he is the main character, too.

The body language of the main character is open to his right (audience left), which would indicate that the three characters in this third are supporting characters. The two who are physically touching are linked in some way, probably romantically. That would then leave the single blonde woman on the far left as the supporting love interest for the main character.

The same ideas can be shown with horizontal lines also.

In the mock-up of an advertising flyer right, the horizontal thirds have been created to guide the audience/readers. There is important text in the top and bottom thirds. This text indicates the date or the title of the event/product, which is what the audience needs to see.

The middle third carries an image of a modern office building with trees around it. This conveys that the event will be both forward looking (the modern build) and sensitive to nature/current issues.

DON'T FORGET

A poster is never just 'put together'. Each element in the image has been chosen and placed with extreme care to detail and the connotations that will be given.

ONLINE TEST

Test your knowledge of print media at www.brightredbooks.net/subjects

THINGS TO DO AND THINK ABOUT

Look at the *vertical* thirds in the Harry Potter poster. What is the audience being drawn to see? What does it suggest about the representation or importance of each of the characters in the poster?

Then, look at how the horizontal thirds are used. How does the poster draw audience's eyes to the important things?

With both questions, use your knowledge of language codes and mise en scène, in other words, everything that you've read through in the Analysis chapters, to guide you.

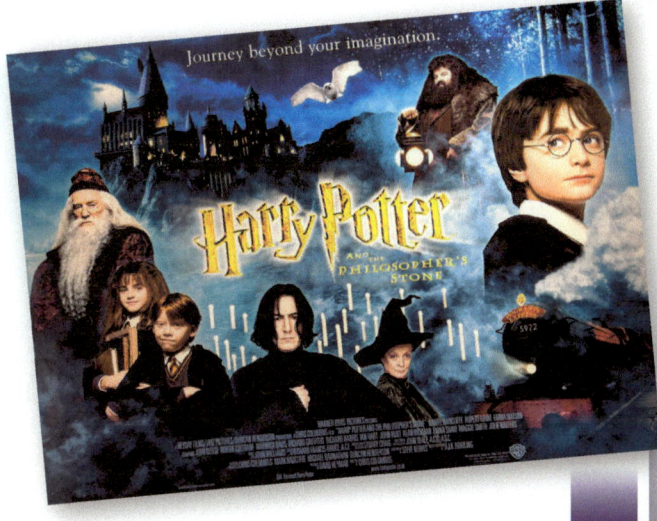

Analysis

REPRESENTATION

PEOPLE, CREATURES, PLACES

Representation discusses how media texts re-present reality in a manner that the audience for the text will accept as being believable and realistic. Representations will be based on the expectations that the audience have of the characters and the settings. They will either meet or challenge these expectations.

DON'T FORGET

The red hair, tartan, Irn-Bru and haggis mentioned have been used so often they have become stereotypes. These are representations that are commonly known but are over-simplified.

DON'T FORGET

It is very important that the use of national stereotypes does not cross the line into racial abuse – which can happen, quite easily, because the representations have become so ingrained in our culture.

ONLINE

Learn more about racist stereotyping by following the link at www.brightredbooks.net/subjects

REPRESENTING PEOPLE

It is important for the plot of a film text that the audience understand that a particular character comes from a particular country. How do you go about it?

Nationalities are a good place to start a discussion about representation as there are some very clear images. For instance, Scots are often shown with red hair and wearing a kilt. They might be drinking Irn-Bru or eating a haggis. When the idea of a Scotsman is suggested to an audience, the audience will expect some of these concepts. By putting them into the re-presentation of a Scots person, the audience's expectations will be met, allowing them to understand the film text more easily.

REPRESENTING CREATURES

If you were given the challenge of representing an alien for a TV programme or a film, how would you go about it?

In the early 1960s, it didn't take much to highlight the differences between people. When Gene Roddenberry launched *Star Trek*, he represented an alien by simply adding a couple of pointy ears onto an actor, and cutting his hair slightly differently. The audiences accepted Mr Spock as an alien, without question: the ears were enough to represent 'ALIEN'.

During the 1970s, Steven Speilberg made the aliens of *Close Encounters of the Third Kind* humanoid, but with longer arms and neck – something recognisable, but more alien than Spock.

More recently, it is not quite as easy. We are more used to people being different, looking different or acting different, and so, in order to represent an alien, something more extreme is needed. Director Neill Blomkamp created something more insect-like for his *District 9* aliens.

As audience expectations have developed, so the need to make stranger looking, sounding and acting aliens has developed, too. The language codes around aliens have changed, too. Spock was shot in normal lighting and costume since the concept of Star Trek was that aliens and humans could live in harmony together. The lighting for *District 9* is darker, suggesting something less friendly. Spock spoke English fluently; the *District 9* Prawns are more guttural and less erudite.

Analysis: People, creatures, places

REPRESENTING PLACES

The same principles of stereotyping can be applied to places, too. *Friends* is a series set in New York (although filmed in Los Angeles). The setting was established by representations of New York. In the opening shots of each episode, long shots of New York's skyline are shown (the shots that featured the World Trade Center towers were removed after September 2001). These meet the audience's expectations – a show set in New York should have street scenes and the iconic skyline.

During the show's run, other New York representations were shown. The most obvious of these was the Yellow Cab that the character Phoebe inherited from her grandmother – a very stereotypical New York thing. New York's sporting teams (particularly the Knicks – the National Basketball Association (NBA) team) are frequently mentioned in dialogue between the male characters.

DON'T FORGET

The key to re-presenting reality to the audience is finding the things that make people, creatures or places recognisable in a simple, easily recognised manner. The creators of media texts will use lighting, costume, body language, cultural codes, editing, camera shots and sound cues/dialogue in order to do this.

THINGS TO DO AND THINK ABOUT

Apart from Scotland, what national stereotypes exist for other nationalities? How about a Frenchman? An Englishman? An American or a Russian? What cultural codes would you use to represent these people?

What geographical representations would be used for an Edinburgh film? Or one set in London, Paris, Beijing?

ONLINE TEST

Test yourself on representation online at www.brightredbooks.net/subjects

ANALYSIS

IDEAS AND EVENTS

IDEOLOGY

An element of representation that features at Higher is the concept of **ideology**. This means the beliefs and **values** that the creating institution hold that become apparent through the texts that are produced.

Those beliefs can be political, social, religious, personal or professional.

Professional

Hollywood director Christopher Nolan, whose recent work includes the Christian Bale Batman trilogy, has stated several times that he does not like using digital effects when he can use real film instead. Nolan has commented: 'However sophisticated your computer-generated imagery [**CGI**] is, if it's been created from no physical elements and you haven't shot anything, it's going to feel like animation.'

This is part of his professional ideology and it filters into his work. He doesn't discount the use of CGI, but wants the experience for the audience to be as real as possible. CGI has to be based on elements of the real world.

One of the more ambitious stunts that Nolan planned for *The Dark Knight* is discussed in the section on External Constraints. However, there are other stunts in that text that demonstrate Nolan's ideology just as well.

For instance, when Christian Bale's Batman jumps from a rooftop in Hong Kong, viewers are watching a stuntman jump from a rooftop – albeit one in America since they were not given permission to film the stunt in Hong Kong. The man jumping is real; the building is the effect.

Social and religious

In 2012, the French satirical magazine *Charlie Hebdo* published a cartoon that showed the Prophet Muhammed naked. On both sides of this event, there were strong ideologies at play.

For many in Islam, it is the highest form of blasphemy to depict the Prophet in any form, but the addition of his nudity was too much to bear. The religious ideology prohibits such a depiction as the Prophet is a sacred figure within the faith.

When Muslims practice art, many of them will not cross the line and depict the Prophet in anything other than words. That is the ideology in action through the media texts that are produced.

On the other hand, the French state has maintained a separation of religion and state since Napoleonic times, and believes in the concept of free speech. The political ideology permits satire at all times, including representations of religious figures considered sacred to others. At the time, even though the French government noted that the timing of the cartoons (following close on the heels of a number of attacks on French embassies in the Middle East) was poor, they defended the right of the magazine to publish.

Away from such stark ideologies, the representation of companies and institutions can be symbolised through a simple image.

However, the panda of WWF means more than just a simple animal under threat from extinction. The connotation attached to the logo covers all animals under threat *and* the work that is going on to try to save them from extinction. The representation that is the logo encapsulates the animals and the beliefs – a simple representation and the ideology mixed together.

Analysis: Ideas and events

EVENTS

Major events and holidays during the calendar year are often represented simply through a picture, sound or symbol. Often this has come about through the symbol itself being used so often that it and the event have become synonymous and a media text need only use the symbol to represent the entire event.

A red heart on a pink and white card connotes Valentine's Day. A red heart represents love at any point in the year, but putting it on a card will create the representation for Valentine's Day.

Earlier on, you looked at the connotations of colour. What connotations would a yellow heart or a blue heart carry if they replaced a red one?

Over the years, research has shown that people prefer to send Christmas cards that depict snow scenes.

These cards are sent even though the odds against a white Christmas are significant. London has a 6 per cent chance, Glasgow a 35 per cent chance and Aberdeen 53 per cent. The snow scene represents Christmas for those who send the cards. The facts don't alter the stereotype or the audience reaction to the representation. A pine tree, covered in snow, is the basic representation of Christmas – even in the Southern hemisphere, where it is summer at Christmas!

P.S. I Love U!

 ONLINE

The concept of Ideology can be investigated more using the link on our Digital Zone www.brightredbooks.net/subjects

 DON'T FORGET

All of us have an ideological 'lens' through which we engage media. It is our upbringing, our political, cultural and religious beliefs (or lack of). These shape the way we read media texts.

 THINGS TO DO AND THINK ABOUT

What are the connotations behind the Starbucks logo? What about the Google logo? Discuss this with your friends and class.

What other calendar events have a simple or complex representation such as the logos or images discussed here? Think about personal events or charity events.

 ONLINE TEST

Test your knowledge of ideas and events at www.brightredbooks.net/subjects

Analysis
NARRATIVE

NARRATIVE STRUCTURES 1

THE STORY BEGINS

Since the first 'Stone Age Banksy' discovered the wonderful properties of charcoal, humankind has been telling stories and recording them for others. In those records, humankind found a need to link the images – to tell a story or a narrative.

When we are presented with images, there is a natural desire to link them. With these images, has the child left the city, gone on a long journey and ended in a more rural setting? Or do they connect another way?

It is a natural human reaction to create a structure around the narratives that we experience.

Over the hundreds of years that we have been telling one another's stories, different people have studied the structures, seeking patterns that are repeated. If a pattern is repeated, then it can be understood, used and manipulated.

Todorov

One such study, conducted by Tzvetan Todorov, has been dubbed **'classic' narrative** structure. In Todorov's studies he saw that narratives follow a simple pattern. A narrative starts with the protagonist in their *Normality* or *Equilibrium*. This is where they are at home – socially, professionally, literally.

Red Riding Hood starts at her house. This is her home, where she feels safe. It is where she gathers the cakes and drink to take to her ill grandmother.

At some point, an event will cause a *disruption* that will destroy the equilibrium and force the protagonist out of their normal comfort zones. It may take some time for the protagonist to identify the cause of the change, allowing for a *recognition of the disruption*, and then an *attempt to fix the disruption*.

Red has to go through the forest, which she knows to be dangerous. She encounters the wolf – who disrupts her plan by tempting her off the path. Her arrival at Grandmother's house and the questions put to the wolf about ears and eyes show that she has recognised the disruption, while the arrival of the woodsman attempts to fix it.

Eventually, the protagonist will overcome whatever odds have been stacked against them, allowing them to return home. However, the events of the narrative and the consequences of the disruption mean that there is a *New Normality* in place. We can never go back, only forwards.

contd

Analysis: Narrative structures 1

The new normality for Red is that she is no longer innocent or (depending on the version and the level of sanitisation it has gone through) that she no longer has a grandmother. Her life has changed profoundly.

Very often, even within a classical structure, it will be very clear that there is a hero and a villain, or that there are two gangs fighting against each other, or that there is something bigger happening and the combined forces of good are going against the combined forces of evil.

Lévi-Strauss

Claude Lévi-Strauss (not to be confused with plain Levi Strauss who invented Levi jeans) also theorised about narrative structure. What he came up with was the need for there to be a *binary opposition*.

His theory suggests that people (the audiences of media texts) engage with texts where there is a clear opposition between two distinct entities or beliefs, as this is how life is viewed by the majority of people. The audience will always be hoping that there will be a manner in which the oppositions will be joined into one by the end of the text.

This does not mean that Todorov's ideas are wrong. In fact, they fit happily together, since it is very likely that some sort of enemy or villain will be responsible for the disruption that takes the protagonist out of their comfort zone – the Wolf versus Red Riding Hood – for example.

So what?

What is important is the mention of the audience engaging with a text.

None of the key aspects of media exist on their own – they integrate with one another.

Example:
A typical Higher exam question will ask you to *analyse how narrative has been influenced* by society, institution or audience. When it comes to narrative structures, it is important to understand how an audience will react to different structures and what they get out of them.

Example:
An audience recognising the classical structure of a text will *expect* to see the protagonist lose their equilibrium, and face significant struggles. However, they will also expect that the protagonist will come out of the text: a happy ending, albeit one that may have sad consequences. It may be that the audience will have to wait to see the structure come to a conclusion. The first trilogy of *Star Wars* films followed this structure across the trilogy. Luke is taken out of his normality by the disruption of the Empire in *Star Wars: Episode IV – A New Hope* (1977). He struggles through that disruption through *Star Wars: Episode V – The Empire Strikes Back* (1980) and only gains a new normality at the end of *Star Wars: Episode VI – Return of the Jedi* (1983).

At the same time, an audience recognising a binary opposition will be guided by the text to support one side or the other (through representations and language codes). The audience is drawn away from the darkness of Darth Vader (music, black costume) towards the light of Luke Skywalker (music, lighter costumes).

ONLINE
Look at this video on our Digital Zone from the MSLGROUP – a global public relations company. It reviews what you've just read through.

DON'T FORGET
Narrative structures can be some of the most straightforward parts of media analysis because we have been using them all our lives.
However, because we are so familiar with them, they can be the aspects that we struggle to see! It is important to practice analysing texts of all kinds – films, adverts, TV programmes, news articles – and deliberately look for the narrative structure in them.

ONLINE TEST
Test your knowledge of narrative structures at www.brightredbooks.net/subjects

THINGS TO DO AND THINK ABOUT

Think of your favourite film (or one that you know very well). Write down a description of what the *Normality* looks like. Then, describe where the *Disruption* occurs. Finally, describe what is different about the *New Normality* that is entered into at the end of the protagonist's journey.

ANALYSIS

NARRATIVE STRUCTURES 2

THE STORY CONTINUES

On pages 22–23, we discussed the need of humans to place a structure around any narrative they engage with, and two of those structures: classical and binary opposition. Through those the tentative use of words like 'hero', 'heroine' and 'villain' was beginning to be seen.

During the early part of the 20th century, the Russian Vladimir Propp analysed 100 Russian fairy tales, to examine if a clear, repeatable narrative structure existed. His work identified eight archetypal characters (Hero, Villain, Princess – and her Father, Donor, Dispatcher, Hero's Helper, False Hero). Often called the *Mythical Structure*, it is possible that different text-specific characters can fulfil more than one of the **archetypes**.

Propp

The *Hero* and the *Villain* are the protagonist and the antagonist. While the names are masculine, it is important to note that the roles themselves are gender neutral and can be fulfilled by male or female characters.

The Hero is set on a quest by the *Dispatcher*, is given 'magic' help by the *Donor* and is assisted throughout the quest by the *Helper*. At the end of the quest, the hero will win the *Princess* or the *Prize* often having negotiated with the *Father of the Princess*.

Finally, somewhere during the narrative, the *False Hero* will make a move, either for the Princess or for the glory that should belong to the Hero for completing the quest.

As mentioned in the last section, the writers of media texts use narrative structure in order to help the audience engage with the text. *Mythical structure* is familiar to the audience as it echoes the fairy tales of childhood. Very quickly, an audience will respond to the needs of the hero, fighting against the villain.

By identifying with characters in the text, the audience will want to know what happens next. They will want to see if the hero escapes the plots of the villain. They may even want to see what cunning plan the villain comes up with.

Joseph Campbell

While Propp proposed a theory that covered Russian fairy tales, American Joseph Campbell proposed the *monomyth,* a narrative theory that covers all myth-based narratives the world over, including some of the major world religions.

It is a surprisingly complex model, and is known by the title *The Hero's Journey* and details the stages of the journey that the hero must face. Roughly speaking, it follows the same path as Todorov's classical theory, but in much, much more detail. The weblink will allow you to start researching for yourself.

At its simplest, Campbell's theory allows for three acts within the text. These are the 'Departure', the 'Initiation' and 'Return'. The hero must depart on the quest, often after a significant amount of pressure and refusal. During the period of initiation, the hero will be tempted (to surrender, to join the enemy, to lose the moral high ground) and will face a number of trials. Once the third act has commenced, the hero must return and face the impact of the quest.

In J. R. R. Tolkien's *The Lord of the Rings*, Frodo (as Hero) only departs on the quest after much persuading from all sides. While on the quest he is tempted to surrender the ring – to use it and become powerful – while also coping with trials of mind and body. Finally, when he and his friends complete their quest, they must come to terms with loss of loved ones – and then cleanse the Shire.

Perhaps the most important point from a contextual point of view is that Campbell's studies have become essential reading for screenwriters in Hollywood. A seven-page edit,

Dorothy is the Hero, with the Wicked Witch as the Villain (at least until her death). The Good Witch is the Dispatcher; she sets the quest for Dorothy to 'Follow the Yellow-brick Road'. The Scarecrow, the Tin Man and the Lion are the Helpers – they assist Dorothy. They, along with the Good Witch, also act as Donors – the hapless three provide Dorothy with what she needs along the road, while the Witch has given Dorothy the shoes of the Wicked Witch: protection and her method of getting home. The Wizard is (initially) the Prize – he has the knowledge to get Dorothy home. He is also the False Hero, claiming to be something that he is not. The Scarecrow, the Tin Man and the Lion, being the representations in Oz of friends that Dorothy has in Kansas, are the father figures, guiding and keeping her safe.

> Hero
> Villain
> Princess...
> ...and her Father
> Donor
> Dispatcher
> Hero's Helper
> False Hero

ONLINE

Learn more about the hero's journey by following the link at www.brightredbooks.net/subjects

contd

Analysis: Narrative structures 2

A Practical Guide to The Hero with a Thousand Faces, was written in the 1970s and evolved into a full book, *The Writer's Journey: Mythic Structure for Writers* (Christopher Vogler).

What that means is that almost any film may have elements of the Hero's Journey built into the script. This is a decision that the creating institution has made, knowing that the fairy-tale/mythic qualities of the Hero, Villain, Helper and so forth will be recognised very quickly by the audience. This recognition will allow the audience access to the preferred reading – the interpretation of the text desired by the institution.

NARRATIVE STRUCTURE IN TELEVISION

When discussing television, it is important to understand the difference between a series and a serial, since these forms dominate the market.

A series is designed in an episodic structure. Each episode is self-contained. In the case of drama or sitcom shows, the characters will not develop much from episode to episode, and any disruptions are dealt with within the time limit of the episode. As a result of this self-contained nature, the episodes can be shown out of production order since there is often little or no continuity between episodes. Think of shows like *Law and Order*, which has successfully run in the US and the UK.

A serial, on the other hand, develops a narrative over several episodes. The audience will expect that the character will solve the disruption and achieve an eventual resolution, although this will not happen until the last episode in the season. More often within a serial, the characters will have a narrative arc – a linear development of the character throughout the season. Episodes of serials need to be watched in order. *Game of Thrones* is an example of this.

Whereas both series and serials conclude with a resolution to the narrative, a third structure, utilised by soap operas, deliberately avoids this. Soaps will run several plot lines simultaneously, involving a number of characters and relationships. At the end of each episode a cliffhanger is created so as to avoid the conclusion to the narrative and to attract the audience to keep watching. A cliffhanger ending is created when the narrative ends suddenly, leaving the fate of the characters (often the hero or, in the case of a soap, a popular character) in doubt. Where there is an episodic narrative structure, the enigma created will hook the audience into watching the next episode.

Individual storylines will reach a resolution, but others are open, keeping the audience's interest. Plot lines are simple and easy to follow and are often repeated with different characters, focusing on community or domestic concerns. UK soaps will often select themes that are current (or have been recently) in order to capitalise on audience interest.

As a TV programme, *Buffy the Vampire Slayer* combines the three typical types of television programmes in order to keep the audience watching.

Series	Every episode tackles a new subject, no impact on rest of series	Most episodes here – monster of the week – closed narrative. Gentlemen come to town, defeated.
Serial	Every episode links into the next	Mystery of the Initiative – Buffy finds out more week by week until grand finale – open until finale
Soap	Focused on relationships/family/problems	Run across seasons/whole series, for example, Buffy's conflict between being Slayer and normal girl, romance with Riley – reward audience loyalty as see characters grow/develop – open narrative

ONLINE

Read up about Vogler's book at www.brightredbooks.net/subjects

DON'T FORGET

There is no official list of 'structures that you need to know' – the ones shown here are the most common and the ones that you will be able to spot most readily in the texts with which you engage.

THINGS TO DO AND THINK ABOUT

Look back at the four pictures in the last chapter (the girl, the road, the city and the fishing village). Using those four pictures create a story that holds them together – something more elaborate than just four, simple sentences.

Did you create a villain? (Maybe a reason for the girl to move house?)
Is there a disruption and then, after a journey, a new normality?

Try it out on friends and family – don't tell them what you are looking for. Show them the four pictures and ask them to tell a story that connects the pictures.

ONLINE TEST

Test your knowledge of narrative structures at www.brightredbooks.net/subjects

ANALYSIS
NARRATIVE CODES 1

WHAT IS NARRATIVE?

When an English teacher talks about the narrative, they are discussing the plot, the story.

When a media teacher talks about narrative, they are meaning the structure (how the plot was constructed); the conventions (what the audience would expect to find in particular narrative forms); and a series of codes (commonly practised elements that symbolise or connote something to the audience).

It's much more than just the story.

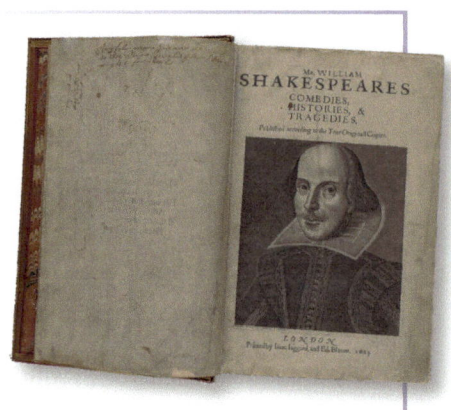

ROLAND BARTHES

When a rich, medieval tapestry is explored in detail, single threads can be selected and tracked across the whole piece, showing where they bring a highlight here and detail there.

As he studied, French literary theorist and philosopher Roland Barthes created a list of narrative codes that he saw as being woven into narratives. These codes, working alongside narrative structures, helped audiences to interpret and even predict the narrative, so making the texts more engaging and enjoyable.

Barthes identified five codes: Hermeneutic (Enigma), Proairetic (Action), Semantic, Symbolic and Cultural.

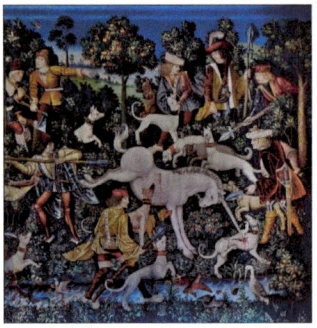

Detail from The Unicorn Tapestries which hang in Stirling Castle

ENIGMA

Taking these one by one, Hermeneutics is the study of texts in order to gain understanding. The name derives from Hermes, the figure of legend who mediated (or interpreted) between the Gods and the mortals on Earth. In media terms, seeking the points of understanding translates as finding the moments of enigma – the moments where there is a puzzle that the audience need to solve.

Television shows have been using this concept since their very earliest point as a way of hooking an audience into watching. The prologue – a short piece before the opening credits that introduces part of the storyline – will not answer any of the 'Big Five' questions (who, what, why, when, where) and so will entice the audience into watching further in order that these enigmas be solved.

Enigmas at the end of programmes have been a constant thread through television history, too. The soap opera (so-called because the first sponsors were soap powders/detergent companies) would be unable to function properly without the 'cliffhanger' ending.

In 1980/1981, the American show *Dallas* took the cliffhanger to new levels of audience interaction as the question, 'Who shot J. R.?' (which was the enigma at the end of the third season, 1979–1980) was sold on T-shirts and other **merchandise**.

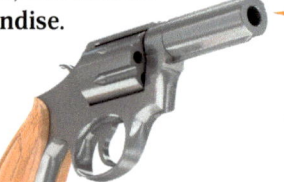

Analysis: Narrative codes 1

ACTION

Proairetic codes (commonly, thankfully, known as Action codes) are often difficult to spot, because we, the audience, are already thinking about the next thing: we did not consciously register the cue that took our brains there.

To explain: an action code is something that the audience would interpret as being the precursor to something else. For instance, a character grasping the door handle (the movement is the action code) would precursor the opening of the door and the character going through it (or someone coming in). Since the follow-on action is so easily interpreted, the conscious registration of the code is missed. Only in absence would an audience miss these codes: a sudden jump cut from interior discussion to exterior walking without the door opening may jar slightly and the audience's understanding of the text would be more limited.

A key factor in all of this is audience expectation. Action codes create expectations that, more often than not, are fulfilled, and a satisfied audience is one that will re-engage with the text on a regular basis.

SEMANTIC

Semantic codes allow for references to be drawn through connotations in word, action or image. For instance, a bone introduced into a text may connote the presence of a dog or of a corpse, depending upon the genre of the piece. On a second level, the connotation or semantic link may refer to something within the text itself.

One particularly famous example of a semantic code is from Stanley Kubrick's *2001: A Space Odyssey*. At the end of the proto-human section of the film, there is a famous match-cut between a thigh bone twirling in the air and a spaceship orbiting Earth. However, as well as being an amazing example of editing, the bone, in the hands of the proto-human, represents a tool: the highest form of technology available to humankind at that point. The spaceship is also a tool of humankind, the highest form of technology that is available and its grace and civilised lines at once link it to and detach it from the bone.

SYMBOLS

Symbolic codes are similar. They apply when an object is being used as a symbol for something else. Where semantic codes are based on the connotations, symbolic codes are direct metaphorical constructs. The proto-human's bone can symbolise a tool and development, while semantically connoting the primitive life.

Music can also work in a symbolic manner. John William's composition *The Imperial March (Darth Vader's Theme)* is used throughout the *Star Wars* franchise as a leitmotif (see earlier) to indicate that the Empire, often in the person of Darth Vader, are about to either come onto the screen or act in some manner. Similarly, a violin string-tone is used by Hans Zimmer to represent the Joker in Nolan's *The Dark Knight*. It is the first musical note struck in the film and remains audible even though the Joker himself is only revealed towards the end of the robbery.

In order to get hold of Narrative Coding, it is important that we develop a 'big picture' point of view and step back from the texts.

Sometimes this can be helped by looking at texts that are not from our culture – other European films/adverts or from further afield across the world. Where there is no innate understanding of the spoken language or the cultural coding, then we are forced to look for narrative codes to help us interpret the text.

 ONLINE

Watch a short video to recap on our Digital Zone – (of course, you could plan your own!).

 DON'T FORGET

This is highly detailed analysis, and can be tricky to get your head around. We take so much for granted in the texts with which we engage, particularly from an action and symbolic point of view.

 ONLINE TEST

Test your knowledge of narrative codes at www.brightredbooks.net/subjects

THINGS TO DO AND THINK ABOUT

Look at the trailer to 2019's *Godzilla: King of the Monsters*.

Enigma, Action, Semiotic and Symbolic codes – it's a treasure hunt!

ANALYSIS
NARRATIVE CODES 2

CULTURAL CODES

These are the same codes that were mentioned back in the chapter on Language – signs that carry a meaning understood by members of a cultural group. This can refer to anything – scientific knowledge, a shared history or a basic understanding of religious ideas. However, for the sake of keeping things simple here, we're going to look at clothing.

Costumes

Costumes can provide enormous cultural value to a text. The audience understands that a person wearing scrubs is medical, whereas blue coveralls would indicate manual labour. A black tricorn hat and an eye patch suggest piratical involvement, while a suit and tie suggest a businessman who is more likely to be trusted (even if his activities are worse than those of the man wearing the eye patch and the funny hat).

The recent ITV drama *Downton Abbey* has shown that costumes can allow audiences to access times that are outside of their own experiences. They have also shown that the social status of characters can be gauged through clothing. The first series was set in the late Edwardian period (the sinking of RMS *Titanic* in 1912 featured) and the Crawley family are made clearly distinct from their staff through their clothing.

Colours

The final strand of cultural coding comes through the use of colour. In the North-Western Hemisphere, an audience will be able to interpret that a female character dressed in white with a (white) veil is about to get married. Equally, a man in a black suit (not a dinner jacket) with a plain black tie may well be going to a funeral. Blue is seen as connoting loyalty; red has power, connoting lust, anger or danger depending on the context.

These are the same as the language codes that were discussed in that chapter. However, when being analysed as cultural codes, colours also need to take national cultures into account.

One simple example of this is red. In the North-West Hemisphere, as mentioned, there is power and passion in red. It connotes lust, anger, danger or love. However, in the Orient, red is the colour of good fortune, which is why Chinese New Year is celebrated with red lanterns and small red-wrapped presents being given to family and friends. A red light hanging outside a building in a Chinese film may represent good fortune. In a British film, it could suggest prostitution. Cultural decoding can lead to embarrassing confusion!

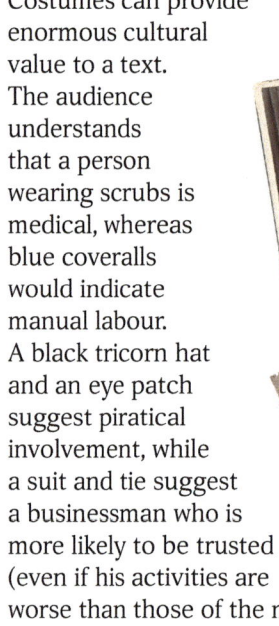

DON'T FORGET

The last chapter suggested that texts from other cultures forced us to watch more closely and actively. Here, through the explanation of cultural coding, we can see what kinds of differential decodings can be created when an audience mis-interprets the narrative codes that are built into the text.

Analysis: Narrative codes 2

 THINGS TO DO AND THINK ABOUT

Watch the opening 50 seconds of the John Wayne film *The Searchers* and follow the list below of the action codes as they happen.

Action (ACT); Enigma (ENG); Symbolic (SYM); Semantic (SEM); Cultural (CUL)

SHOT 1

Text: 'TEXAS 1868' on a dark blue background.

CUL: TEXAS – gives the geographical location.

CUL: 1868 – gives historical location. Three years after Civil War – which is important information in terms of the relations between characters.

Music: Shifts from initial menacing bars to peaceful violin ballad that threads through the opening shots.

SEM: Menace
SEM: Peacefulness

Dissolve to Shot 2

SHOT 2

The frame is completely black; the blackness is partially peeled away from left to right revealing a shadowed skirted figure, outlined from the back against bright light and yellow colour that is gradually perceived to be desert – plateau rocks, scrub and so forth.

ACT: To open a door
ACT: To begin to tell a story
CUL: 19th-century female dress
SYM: Oppositions of light/dark – nature/home
ENG: Who is the woman?

The woman's right hand, which was grasping the door, drops to her side as she walks forward. The camera tracks behind her.

ACT: To walk through the door

The woman walks forward and to the right of the frame. As she walks, she emerges into colour and is seen to be wearing a blue dress with a pair of white straps (of an apron?) crossed over the back.

SEM: Domesticity, in terms of colour blue (loyalty also). Blue also links the woman with Ethan, rather than her husband, Aaron, who wears red.

With her right hand, the woman grasps a post that has emerged into the shot as the result of the camera's track and right pan. Both the camera and the woman then remain stationary. Her clothes flutter.

SEM: Wind

The camera pans right, aligning its visual field with the woman's.

ACT: To look into the distance

Gradually, a horseman appears in centre frame, middle distance.

ACT: To see someone
ENG: Who is the horseman?

SHOT 3

A frontal shot of the woman standing with her right hand on the post. Behind her, is a brick wall in which there is a framed space, split by a post, through which the landscape reappears.

CUL: Architecture of the house – pioneer simplicity
CUL: Home vs desert
ENG: Is there a link between the horseman and the woman?

The woman lifts her hand to her forehead, shading her eyes.

ACT: To attempt to identify
SEM: Glare from the sun

 VIDEO LINK

Find the clip for the opening scene of The Searchers at www.brightredbooks.net/subjects

 ONLINE TEST

Test your knowledge of narrative codes at www.brightredbooks.net/subjects

29

Analysis

CATEGORIES

GENRE AND PURPOSE

WHAT IS GENRE?

Genre typically refers to the type of narrative (and narrative structure) that is used within the text. For example, 'Horror' genre aims to tap into the audience's primal instincts: survival. It seeks to create discomfort and fear by placing the audience in unnatural positions where people, objects or even nature itself act in strange and unexpected ways. By contrast, 'Romantic Comedy' seeks to reassure audiences through having characters join together through humorous plot twists, finishing with a 'happy ending' where everyone lives happily ever after.

IS THERE A LIST?

There is no 'set list' of genres. Wikipedia suggests that there are at least 21, although many of those have sub-genres attached to them. Equally, genres can be combined, creating another: 'Romantic Comedy' is a combined genre, as is Simon Pegg and Nick Frost's 2004 Zombie offering *Shaun of the Dead*, which describes itself as a Zom-Rom-Com, combining zombie horror, romance and comedy.

The most common genres are Romance, Sci-Fi, Thriller, Action, Horror, Fantasy and Comedy. In each of these, there are certain Genre Markers. These are the objects, themes and even people whose presence tells the audience what they are watching.

GENRE MARKERS

Romance	Sci-Fi	Thriller	Action	Horror	Fantasy	Comedy
Couple who are parted	Technology	Villain and (unlikely) hero	Resourceful character	Strange people	Nature	Humour through situation
One must have a secret	Futuristic setting	Hero will be threatened	Fight and chase sequences	Strange objects	Medieval setting	Uses satire or parody
Focus on relationship	Man v Tech	Suspense	Guns and explosions	Storms	Man v Nature	Humour through people
Happy ending	Space/Aliens	Hero will win at the end of the day	Crisis solved and hero beats villain	Gothic House	Legendary/Mythical beasts	Happy ending – little or no tragedy

The distinction between genre conventions and narrative conventions is a slender one. So, while a narrative convention may shrink time within a science-fiction story, a genre convention for science fiction would require that there be some technology that is beyond the ability of the contemporary society to replicate.

In a film text that can be categorised as 'Action', the genre conventions require the hero to be unassuming (and/or even unwilling); that there will be at least one, if not two or three, explosive car chases; and that the hero and villain will face off twice – with the villain winning the first (to create suspense) and then losing the second, giving victory to the hero.

Analysis: Genre and purpose

PURPOSE

Purpose describes the reasons why the text was created in the first place. There is a baseline, default answer to this: profit (or money at the very least). Most media texts are created with some kind of profit motive in mind. However, this is not entirely true of all texts.

Beyond that, purpose often falls into three points: inform, educate or entertain.

When the purpose is to inform, then there is instruction – the passing on of information – without a specific need for the audience to act. When the purpose is to educate, then the information is passed to the audience with a specific desire that they act upon it.

A documentary, for example, will have the purpose to inform the audience. There is no assumption on the part of the creating institution that the audience will watch it and take any action based on the information that they have learned.

On the other hand, government information films – like the videos used to teach children the Green Cross Code – have a purpose to educate the audience. The creating institution makes an assumption that the audience will learn and take action on the information they have been given.

In more art-related media (performance arts, films, television, writing, portraiture and the like) the purpose of the text is more likely to be entertainment for the audience. There is no information of any value being passed onto the audience.

With commercial adverts, there is often a mix of purposes. Adverts entertain the audience while educating them about some product or service. There is a hope of creating profit through persuading the audience to act (purchase the product or service) but it will only happen if the audience feel properly entertained.

ONLINE

Watch the YouTube clip on our Digital Zone, where the vlogger has edited the first Harry Potter film, *Harry Potter and the Philosopher's Stone*, into trailers for seven different genres. Not only does this highlight the markers used for genres, but also revises the concept of editing from earlier!

DON'T FORGET

In order to appeal to as wide an audience as possible, most moving image texts will incorporate more than one genre into the text. There will be rom-com and sci-fi wrapped up together, as this will appeal to both a male and a female audience (generally speaking).

THINGS TO DO AND THINK ABOUT

1. Select a film or TV programme that you know well. Describe what changes would need to be made (to characters, lighting, sets and so on) in order to change the genre.
2. Watch the clip on the Digital Zone. It is the 2011 John Lewis Christmas advert. The purpose of the advert is to boost profits at John Lewis. Think through *how* this advert entertains the audience and how it educates the audience (about the range of things that can be bought at John Lewis).

ONLINE TEST

Test your knowledge of purpose and genre at www.brightredbooks.net/subjects

ANALYSIS

FORM, MEDIUM, STYLE, TONE AND MORE

FORM AND MEDIUM

The *medium* and *form* of a text are linked closely together. Medium describes the general method through which the text is being communicated: Print, Web, Radio, TV and Optical Disc (although this is not an exhaustive list). The form then describes the subset of the medium. So, medium is print, and the form can be newspaper, novel, non-fiction, textbook and so on.

Medium	Form
Print	Letter, newspaper, magazine, poster, encyclopaedia, novel
Web	website, Twitter, links, blogs, social media
Radio	Audio drama, breakfast show, drive time, music, news
Film	Television, feature film, YouTube, viral
Optical drive	CD/Blu-ray/DVD

The medium and form may seem to be straightforward, and they are often the first to be identified in an analysis. However, they can also influence the range of technical codes (see Language chapter).

To explain further, a magazine like *Marie Claire* or *Vogue* (medium is print, form is fashion magazine) will make more use of lighting and colour connotations than will a production of *The Times* or *The Sun* (where the medium is print and the form is newspaper).

STYLE

The Style of a media text can vary dramatically and will depend upon the technical codes employed. For instance, photographs printed in sepia inks can be said to have an 'old-fashioned' style, while the works of artists like Dali and Dada have a surreal style.

As with so much in media analysis, the target audience has a lot to do with the style chosen by the creating institution. A younger audience will prefer something with a more modern style (fast pace, unusual camera angles), whereas an older audience will, normally, prefer something slower, and with more conventional use of cameras, allowing them time to understand the narrative. This style could be termed 'old fashioned'.

A conventional style will follow the normal patterns expected for the genre. A conventionally styled crime film will feature a detective or police officer who is a renegade or maverick character. There will be something personal in the case that prompts the detective to act. The villain will taunt the detective, only to fall by the end of the film.

TONE

The tone is tied closely to style and genre. There is no list of words (as normal) to describe tone and, in fact, tone introduces one of the quirkier aspects of media analysis: *your opinion is right if you can back it up from the text*. Just to repeat that (with a different emphasis) – in media analysis, *as long as you can fully justify your opinion using the text, your answer will be accepted*.

Any list of tone words covers a wide range of adjectives: happy, sad, angry, comedic, sorrowful, harsh, bland, euphoric and so forth. All would be acceptable if something in the text suggests that they are appropriate. The genre will provide a clue to the audience.

For instance, it is unlikely that a romantic comedy will have a sorrowful or depressed tone, while a Disney animation will avoid a realistic tone. Hand in hand with the genre, the tone will tell the audience what to expect from the narrative.

contd

ONLINE

Look at the helpful YouTube video on our Digital Zone regarding how the tone of a text can be established and manipulated.

Analysis: Form, medium, style, tone and more

Tone can be created through lighting, props, societal context and so forth. There is no specific list, but many things can affect the tone of a text. Tone can be set out at the beginning of the text, but can also change during the text, which would leave the audience emotionally engaged in a different manner from the one they started off with.

FURTHER CATEGORIES – OR HOW TO ATTRACT AUDIENCES

Beyond genre, style and tone there are as many ways to categorise texts as there are texts themselves. For instance, very often in the advertising for a film or television text, the previous film work of the director or the producers will be noted.

This technique creates a category that is specific to the director or the producers. For an audience, the fact that a new release is a 'Steven Spielberg' film will carry some weight. The category has connotations attached to it: connotations that designate the quality, style and perhaps even the likely narrative structure of the text.

In this particular instance, Spielberg has a particular reputation for working with, and getting the best out of, child actors. Audiences coming to a Spielberg film would, therefore, expect to find a child actor as one of the main **stars** (and may even mark them for future stardom – Drew Barrymore (*E.T. the Extra-Terrestrial*), Haley Joel Osment (*A.I. Artificial Intelligence*), Dakota Fanning (*War of the Worlds*) and Christian Bale (*Empire of the Sun*) have been directed by Spielberg).

At other times, categories may extend as far as a director and actor working together. For instance, Martin Scorsese (director) and Robert De Niro (actor) have collaborated eight times since the 1970s. Some of their films are recognised as being among the best films of all time. They are typically of the crime genre, and this is something that a potential audience would expect.

A similar relationship exists between Johnny Depp and Tim Burton, which has now reached nine films. These films tend to be humorous, but in a dark manner – there is always something 'not quite right' about the characters that Depp plays. These films do not share genre. *Sweeney Todd: The Demon Barber of Fleet Street* and *Sleepy Hollow* are horror, while *Alice in Wonderland* is fantasy. That quirky characterisation is a Depp trademark and is one of the reasons why audiences are attracted to his films.

Some moving image texts act as *star vehicles* – a category that transcends genres. These are texts that have been created to specifically showcase the style, talents or career of a particular person.

Famously, in Hollywood terms, *The Wizard of Oz* was created specifically for Judy Garland, as a showcase of the young star's talents. Equally, the play (and then film) *Little Voice* was written as a vehicle to show off the vocal talents of Jane Horrocks who can sing like many different stars – including Judy Garland. Comedians like Jerry Seinfeld and Roseanne Barr have had their own comedy shows, featuring them in lead roles, often with semi-auto-biographical storylines.

In each of these cases, the text has been designed to intrigue an audience and engage them with a particular star's career. Often they are the vehicle that launches the career (as is the case with Garland and Horrocks) or enhances it (as is the case with the comedians). Either way, the audience's direct engagement with the star is the purpose of the text.

 **DON'T FORGET**

Although we have mentioned specific categories here, there is no final list that should be memorised or learned. Just as a bag of sugar could be categorised in many ways in a supermarket (baking products, beverages, special offer, spare stock, white powders and so forth) so media texts can be categorised in many different ways and, as with so much else, if you can *justify* your answer using evidence from the text to support yourself, then you will be able to access the marks.

 THINGS TO DO AND THINK ABOUT

Initially using the categories listed above, categorise this group of films and television programmes. There are many categories – from production company through to actors and writers. Each category has at least two entries.

Once that has been achieved, think through any other categories that you could use.

Doctor Who; Sherlock; The Sarah Jane Adventures; Dangerous; Pointless; The Adventures of Tintin; Star Trek into Darkness; The Hobbit.

 ONLINE TEST

Test your knowledge of categories at www.brightredbooks.net/subjects

Analysis

AUDIENCE

AUDIENCE DEMOGRAPHICS/MODE OF ADDRESS

TARGETING AN AUDIENCE

Target audiences, by their nature, represent sweeping generalisations in terms of class, gender, age, education, social grouping and other demographic categories. Each of these classifications is called a demographic.

As an example, consider the adverts that accompanied Coca-Cola's introduction of the Coke Zero product. They featured Wayne Rooney, the footballer. Research had shown that Diet Coke as a product was not popular with men because of the word 'Diet'. The word was removed, and a masculine representation was set up targeting a male demographic.

A text being created will have a focused target audience in mind. Others will engage with the text and enjoy it, but there will be a demographic for whom the text has been specifically designed.

Coke targeted a specific gender demographic, but the text can be designed to target a wider and less specific demographic.

Volkswagen and the super bowl

In 2011, Volkswagen (VW) spent just over $6 million to book a 60 second spot for this advert at the Super Bowl half-time (this does not include the money spent making it).

As a film text, this has a very specific target audience: those who grew up with *Star Wars* – people in their mid-/late 30s and early 40s. Those people are likely married and have a family. They will want to protect that family. Not surprisingly, those are the people in the advert. Anyone older will not understand the *Star Wars* references. Anyone younger will not be in the family or financial position to want a VW car.

VW have targeted a demographic that includes both genders, and has a wide age spread.

Friends

The long-running and ever-popular sitcom *Friends* maintained a very specific target demographic throughout its ten-year run on television.

As with the VW advert, the people in the text give a very real clue as to the **demographics** that the producers were wanting to target. The characters of *Friends* are in their mid-20s (when the show started, running to mid-30s by the time the run ended). This is the age demographic, while they appeal to a mixed gender, being split three to three.

The cast are from different backgrounds, including Italian and New York Jewish, and they represent different faith-streams – Jewish, Roman Catholic and New Age. These represent demographics that cover a large percentage of the desired television audience. However, a lot has been made of the gaps in the demographic – Asian and African-American.

This one sitcom then managed to appeal to as broad a range of target audience as possible.

VIDEO LINK

Watch the advert at www.brightredbooks.net/subjects

CLASS DISTINCTION AND DEMOGRAPHICS

A significant amount of time, energy and research is spent every year examining target audiences and target markets. There is a set of classifications that are used to delineate the different social levels that audiences come from.

In the UK, Social Grade A refers to the upper middle class, B refers to the middle class and C1 refers to lower middle class. All these are professional social grades. C2 and D classify manual workers (skilled or semi-skilled), and E allows for the lowest level of subsistence income (pensioners and casual labour).

Advertising and programming are planned and based around these social grades. Over the last few affluent years, the UK has seen a rise in the ABC1 grouping, which has resulted in changes across the media landscape (as institutions respond to the needs of society). This can be seen through characters of soap operas like ITV's *Coronation Street* or BBC's *Eastenders*, who have changed to fit more into ABC1 and have moved away from the lower socio-economic groups that were once more prevalent.

MODE OF ADDRESS

Staying with *Friends*, the manner in which the characters present themselves to the audience is an *indirect* **mode of address**. This means that the characters do not break what is known as the 'fourth wall' – the screen – that divides them from the audience. Instead, it is as if the audience are hidden as they are looking in on the lives of the characters.

Equally, although there are often storylines that continue from episode to episode, most often an episode of *Friends* requires no specific knowledge from the audience in order to be understood or enjoyed. This means that it also has a *general* mode of address.

Conversely, a David Attenborough series, like *Planet Earth II*, will have the narration directed at the audience. Attenborough will use inclusive pronouns like 'you' and 'us'. He is talking to each individual watching the programme and so has a **direct** mode of **address**.

Although he explains as much as he can, Attenborough's nature series do expect that the audience have a basic understanding of life on Earth and the concept of evolution. There is possibly also an assumption that basic geography and geology is understood. This means that a series like *Planet Earth II* has a *specific* mode of address also.

 ONLINE

Look at the YouTube clip on our Digital Zone from an AS media student explaining how to appeal to an audience.

 **DON'T FORGET**

It is vital for a text that it not only appeal to an audience, but that the audience is reached and their needs met.
That way, audiences will be entertained, and the reason for the text being created in the first place will be justified.

 THINGS TO DO AND THINK ABOUT

Choose one of the events in List 1, below, and then do some short research into how you would advertise the event to the audiences in List 2.

List 1 – Events	List 2 – Audiences
Six Nations Rugby	Teenagers
The Edinburgh International Festival	20s
1980s rock tribute concert	Elderly people
Red Arrows display	Single mothers

 ONLINE TEST

Test your knowledge of audience demographics and mode of address at www.brightredbooks.net/subjects

ANALYSIS

READINGS OF A TEXT

VIDEO LINK

Check out the advert for the Green Cross Code at www.brightredbooks.net/subjects

PREFERRED READING

When an institution puts a media text together, there is a *preferred reading* that they intend the audience to take away with them.

The Green Cross Code has been used in the UK for a number of years to help children learn how to cross a road safely.

This advert (used from 1997 to 2008), complete with singing hedgehogs, has a clear purpose: to educate the public (there is an expectation that action will be taken by the audience).

Public information films (PIFs) are rich sources of text that have a clear preferred reading.

In the example above, the decision was made to produce a catchy song with a cute animation, designed to capture the imagination (and memory) of the target audience – children.

The hedgehogs are a more recent part of a long-running series of road safety PIFs, dating back to the 1950s. With each new version of the PIF, a new character has been created in order to appeal to children. Tufty Fluffytail, a red squirrel, helped teach the message from the 1950s through to the mid-1970s, after which the Green Cross Code Man – a superhero with a particular focus for his powers – took over. The Green Cross Code Man (played by Darth Vader's body actor, David Prowse MBE) ran until about 1990, when the singing hedgehogs were employed. More recently, the alien Ziggy has been learning about crossing the road safely.

The preferred reading of the hedgehog text is that there are certain things they can (must) do in order to ensure safety when crossing the road.

DIFFERENTIAL DECODING

When an audience interprets, or reads, the text in a different way from the manner in which the creators intend, then there is a differential decoding created.

A favourite wedding song (according to any number of lists) is 'Every Breath You Take', by The Police (1983).

Sting, the writer of the song, has commented that he is worried about or disturbed by people who have this as their wedding song.

To him, as the creating institution, the preferred reading is that someone is stalking another person: it is a song about stalking, about taking control of someone. Yet, for many, it is a love song about how, no matter where the person is, they will be watched over and cared for.

Negotiated decoding

There is a particular sub-group of differential decoding called a *negotiated decoding* that allows for the audience to accept some of the preferred reading, but reject other aspects in favour of another interpretation. This might occur while the audience engages with, for instance, a nature documentary.

The BBC/Discovery Channel series *Africa* was presented by David Attenborough. The last episode, *Africa: The Future*, allowed Attenborough the opportunity to expound his own feelings and beliefs regarding the future of the planet, the problems that humans are creating and the need to stop being so destructive towards our environment. It is a very personal viewpoint, and ends with Attenborough face-to-face with a baby rhino that was born blind.

THINGS TO DO AND THINK ABOUT

Go to our Digital Zone to watch the YouTube clip showing the problems of communicating with people using emojis.

Differential decoding could, so easily, happen.

Using the five emojis that are highlighted in the video, write a message to a friend and demonstrate how the message would change across different platforms.

ONLINE

For lyrics of the song, go to www.brightredbooks.net/subjects

VIDEO LINK

Check out the clip of David Attenborough and the baby rhino at www.brightredbooks.net/subjects.
As you watch this clip, remember that Attenborough is recognised across the world as one of the most well-known and respected naturalists. Audiences who engaged with the series may well have accepted the preferred reading for the series – that nature is spectacular and needs careful preservation – but may not accept this last episode because it is so very personal and more specific.

DON'T FORGET

Remember that we have said before that the key aspects of media are integrated – they do not exist on their own or as separate entities.
In order to create the preferred reading, many aspects of language coding/representation/narrative are used to *anchor* the meaning for the audience.

ONLINE TEST

Test your knowledge of readings at www.brightredbooks.net/subjects

Analysis
INSTITUTION

INTERNAL CONSTRAINTS

WHAT CAN YOU CONTROL?

There are problems, issues and rules *within* the institution that is creating the media text that need to be overcome if success is to be achieved. Because these issues are within the company itself, they are issues that can be controlled.

There is no exhaustive list of such events; however, it includes such things as technology, casting, the need to find locations for filming, designing and constructing sets and even feeding and housing the cast and crew.

As an example of this, there is a famous video clip from the set of George Lucas's 1977 epic *Star Wars*. The man who had been hired to be Darth Vader was British actor David Prowse MBE. Ever the professional, he learned the lines and spoke them through the full Vader mask.

VIDEO LINK

Hear Darth Vader's original voice at www.brightredbooks.net/subjects

The problem of Prowse's strong West Country accent was a constraint. He did not sound scary – quite the opposite in fact. Lucas solved the problem by hiring a little-known stage actor, James Earl Jones, to read in the lines, and Vader entered history.

OTHER CHALLENGES

Star Wars also provides a good example of how technology was creating a constraint, and how it was solved by George Lucas.

Prior to Lucas starting to film *Star Wars*, the special effects industry was working well, but had a problem when filming the complex effects shots that Lucas wanted.

ONLINE

Learn more about the process of compositing at www.brightredbooks.net/subjects

In order to make these shots work correctly, the camera would have to pass over the models in *exactly the same manner*, time after time, building up the layers required. Such accuracy was not possible, which left a tell-tale blue shimmer around each effect. This shimmer was what Lucas wanted to remove.

This process is called *compositing*.

His solution, through the genius of the people employed to make those effects, was to create *new technology* that solved the problem. An entirely new system, that guided the camera's motions through a computer, and so repeated the process *exactly the same way* time after time, was designed to remove the blue shimmer and make the effects more realistic.

What is important to remember is that a constraint really is just a production issue, and it should be overcome in order for the production to go ahead.

When a text is being analysed or discussed, then identifying the production issues that have been overcome, like casting, or the lack of technology, is only half the story. The manner in which the issue was dealt with is the other half. This applies in the Assignment that is externally marked as much as for any professional text.

Analysis: Internal constraints

HOW MUCH CAN YOU BUY?

Working through a budget is vital for a production. Everything has to be paid for, one way or another, and there seems no end of things that have to be paid for!

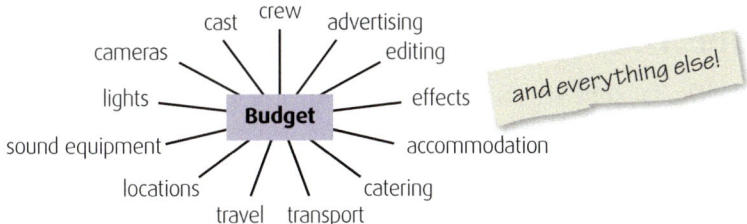

When an idea for a media text (film, advert, theatre, novel and so forth) is in the process of being brought into life, then one of the first things looked for is money. From a film media point of view, this is the *Producer*.

This may be an individual or a company, but they are the one responsible for financing the project and ensuring that it becomes profitable at the other end, once it has been released to an audience.

This means advertising, and that may start long before the final text is ready, so that the target audience gets as much warning as possible. It can be a costly exercise. In order to book a 30-second spot during *The X Factor* final (at Christmas) the producers need to pay some £200,000 (the normal cost is close to £130,000 for prime-time advertising). Most adverts last for a minute.

In America, the prime advert spot on television is during half-time at the Super Bowl. Adverts there cost $5 million per 30 seconds.

To finish off this section where we started, George Lucas's budget for *Star Wars* was the highest budget ever for a film (up to that point). His producers gave him $11 million, but with the technology and effects, he still needed to make cuts. Some of those cuts came in salaries.

He, as director, only took half the salary he was due. Alec Guinness, an Oscar-winning A-list actor, took less, but accepted a percentage of the profits instead. The main three actors were relatively unknown, which allowed for them to have significantly smaller salaries (even though they had the most screen-time). They also made a deal to receive (smaller) percentages of the profits.

For instance, if considering the casting of a text, the constraint may be that the institution cannot afford a well-known star.

This can be seen as an *opportunity* for unknown actors to achieve some kind of fame; a *solution* could be for the institution to use stock footage of other actors. It is not enough to just note the problem; you must investigate the solutions further.

 **DON'T FORGET**

When looking at or writing about Internal Constraints, you should look for the opportunities in or solutions to the situations or problems that present themselves.

 ## THINGS TO DO AND THINK ABOUT

Read the following scenario.

She looked out of the window. The rain trickled down in spaghetti-strands. Boredom seemed to hang in the air.

Something caught her eye – a light in the distance.
Someone was walking across the moor. 'In this weather?' she thought to herself.
She watched, fascinated, and then realised that the light was coming towards her house.

Her house was warm, well-lit; wooden panels on the wall reflected the warmth of the open fire, and the cushions and soft furnishings glowed red in the light from the same flames.

Her attention was suddenly diverted. The phone was ringing.

Plan through a film version of the scenario, listing and taking into account the internal constraints that you would face. Come up with solutions to production problems; look for opportunities to do something different.

 ONLINE TEST

Test your knowledge of institutional constraints at www.brightredbooks.net/subjects

ANALYSIS

EXTERNAL CONSTRAINTS

THE STUFF YOU CAN'T CONTROL – BUT HAVE TO MANAGE

The clip on the Digital Zone shows the flipping of an articulated truck during a chase sequence from Christopher Nolan's *The Dark Knight*. The actual flip was shot without CGI (Nolan's preference). It is a real truck, performing a real flip on a real street.

When Nolan planned this stunt, he faced a number of *external constraints*. These are constraints that are not under the direct control of the producing institution, but present production issues all the same.

It's never been done before

Nolan was facing the fact that no one had ever performed this stunt before, and with good reason: it is incredibly difficult and dangerous. So, there needed to be a system in place to make sure that it happened. An explosive ram was put into the back of the truck that would fire at the right time, hit the ground and push the truck into the air.

The team experimented and concluded that it would work, as long as the truck was facing forward and was straight.

Laws and regulations

The film was being shot in Chicago, specifically the business district where all the banks have their head offices. The team representing Chicago pointed out to Nolan and his stunt team all the points at which there was access to the tunnels and vaults for these businesses all along the street. They were told that there was only one road that they could perform the stunt on without setting off every alarm in the street: they needed to be very precise.

There are health and safety rules in place to protect people at work. When describing a truck that is flipping over after an explosive charge has detonated, then there are concerns about the person who is driving the truck and making sure it is running absolutely straight. This would mean that the cab of the truck would have to be modified with protection around the cab, along with the normal protection for a stunt driver.

City regulations, national laws and, indeed, the laws of physics are all areas that are not within the control of the makers of media texts. They are, however, production issues that need to be overcome. In the case of *The Dark Knight* they were overcome and with great success.

It is not only film media that has problems with laws and regulations. Those who produce print media are also under the guidance of the law, as a recent story from Nottingham shows.

The city council produced a number of posters in an effort to clamp down on begging in the city streets – but the adverts had to be removed because it was felt that they showed homeless people in a negative light.

Working with Mother Nature

No production team can plan around nature. It is unpredictable and potentially hazardous whether it is the weather, plants or animals that are involved.

When George Lucas was filming in Tunisia for *Star Wars*, the desert conditions were so hot that Anthony Daniels, who plays the droid C-3PO, was overheating in his metallic costume. Even in the 1970s, when there was less attention paid to health and safety as part of any process, it was recognised that there needed to be a solution found in order to keep the actor able to work.

The solution was simple – Daniels was filmed from the waist up (whenever possible), to allow him to be bare-legged.

contd

VIDEO LINK

Check out the clip from *The Dark Knight* at www.brightredbooks.net/subjects

ONLINE

Read more about the Nottingham city council posters at www.brightredbooks.net/subjects

Analysis: External constraints

One of the most famous wildlife documentary extracts is David Attenborough's 1978 encounter with gorillas. It was part of the ground-breaking *Life on Earth* series, which launched Attenborough into the public's attention and first showcased the skills of the BBC's Natural History Unit.

Attenborough sat close to a family of gorillas – something that is now no longer allowed – so close that they started to play with him. Two of the young gorillas started to try to remove one of his shoes. Eventually, Attenborough can be seen lying in the bush with a gorilla all but lying on him.

There is no sense of danger, although unquestionably the gorillas are highly dangerous creatures, but there was a need (according to the script) for Attenborough to be explaining the evolutionary aspects of opposable thumbs. The production issue was overcome by simply filming and leaving the script to be filled in as a voice-over once the team were safely back in the studio.

While the aim is always to overcome production issues, sometimes, defeat has to be admitted completely.

In September 2016, the seventh series of the very popular programme *Game of Thrones* had to be delayed because filming could not continue – the weather was too warm to effectively represent winter. In this case, the release date for the series would be pushed back to allow the production team the time that they need to complete the filming.

DON'T FORGET

By their very nature, it is important to acknowledge in your own productions that some external constraints cannot be changed or overcome: school rules, financial constraints, weather and so forth.

Fans will be disappointed, but, sometimes, the external constraints cannot be overcome.

In your analyses, you should always look for evidence of where these constraints have affected the text: a change in plan, a delayed production, an altered narrative.

THINGS TO DO AND THINK ABOUT

In the last chapter, you were asked to read the following scenario.

She looked out of the window. The rain trickled down in spaghetti-strands. Boredom seemed to hang in the air.

Something caught her eye – a light in the distance.
Someone was walking across the moor. 'In this weather?' she thought to herself.
She watched, fascinated, and then realised that the light was coming towards her house.

Her house was warm, well-lit; wooden panels on the wall reflected the warmth of the open fire, and the cushions and soft furnishings glowed red in the light from the same flames.

Her attention was suddenly diverted. The phone was ringing.

This time, you should take into account any external factors that would come into play when attempting to film this scenario. What new production issues would come up? What different solutions would you find?

ONLINE TEST

Test your knowledge of institutional constraints at www.brightredbooks.net/subjects

ASSESSMENT

EXTERNAL ASSESSMENT 1

ONLINE

Remember – the SQA website (www.sqa.org.uk) has up to the last three years' worth of past papers. These are not locked documents, and are available on the public website. That said, Diet 2019 is the first of a new-look Higher paper (accommodating the removal of the mandatory units) so the old papers will look different.

PAPER 1 ANALYSIS OF MEDIA CONTENT

Questions 1 and 2

Questions 1 and 2, which are worth 20 marks each, will ask you to analyse content in terms of a context (or vice versa) through the question stem. Each question has an (a) and a (b) part, which are worth 10 marks each.

The stem of Question 1 will focus on context in terms of content; Question 2 will focus on content and its relationship with context.

You should answer using media texts that you have studied during the year in class. However, you should not feel limited to writing about only one text.

Sample questions

A possible Question 1 might read:

> 1. *How audiences respond to media content can depend on the extent to which key aspects such as categories and/or narrative and/or representations have been used to construct the content.*
>
>   *Analyse how this statement applies to media content you have studied. In your response you should:*
>
>   **(a)** *Analyse the ways in which different audiences might respond to the media content.* 10
>
>   **(b)** *Analyse the ways in which these responses might depend on the use of categories and/or narrative and/or representations.* 10

The 'stem' of the question – the opening paragraph – gives clear guidance as to which key aspects are required to be discussed. Here it is audiences (context) and categories and/or narrative and/or representations (content) that should be the focus.

Alternatively, Question 1 could focus on Institution (internal constraints, external constraints, budgeting, production issues/values and so forth) or Society (time, place, history, events, politics, technology and so on).

Question 1(a) and 2(a) are designed to allow candidates to show the breadth of their knowledge. All the elements of the key aspect of audience can be brought to bear here. In the example above, target audiences, audience reactions/expectations, preferred reading/differential decoding and mode of address. Question 1(b) allows for the same breadth, but across a range of key aspects of content.

Question 2 will be similar in design, but it will deal with *the key aspects that have not yet been discussed*. The breadth of knowledge would be shown through a key aspect of content. In the example below, this would be Language, which would allow candidates to write about lighting, camera shots, camera angles, editing, sound and so on.

Thus, Question 2 would be:

> 2. *How language codes have been used in the construction of media content can be influenced by society and/or institutional factors.*
>
>   *Analyse how this statement applies to media content you have studied. In your response you should:*
>
>   **(a)** *Analyse the ways in which language codes have been used for the construction of media content.* 10
>
>   **(b)** *Analyse the ways in which society and/or institutional factors have influenced the use of language codes.* 10

contd

Between both questions, all seven of the key aspects of media literacy will be covered, although you will be able to focus on certain ones in each question. What that means is that you will be able to use the spread of texts that you have studied through the year. It may well be that one of the texts that you studied lends itself more easily to narrative and representation and another to institution and audience.

Use your texts wisely. Don't get caught up in trying to answer everything from one text.

Whatever texts you decide to use, the absolute requirement is that the answers be *specific* and *detailed*. Answers *must* make specific reference to media texts. It is not enough to suggest that there is a stereotyped representation of an American in a film; candidates *must* describe where in the text the stereotype occurs (*specific*), and how the representation has been created (e.g. language codes, cultural codes, mise en scène). This makes the answer *detailed*.

So, for example, where it is well known that Darth Vader from the *Star Wars* films wears all black to represent evil, it needs to be detailed and specific, thus …

> *When he is first introduced on screen in* The Empire Strikes Back, *Darth Vader is seen as a very imposing character. First, the music – The Imperial March – signals his arrival. It is a blaring brass piece, indicating power and military might. Our first sight of him is the back of his head; there is a sense of mystery created, which is extended by the long shot that follows, showing the whole bridge area of his ship, and Vader standing alone at the viewport. He is solitary, an indication of power …*

… would be a good way of starting your answer to 2(a).

Timing is something that will impact on your answers. You have two and a half hours for this paper and there are three questions to answer. You should aim to split your time evenly between the three sections. This means you have around fifteen minutes for reading and planning your answers and 45 minutes per section. For Questions 1 and 2, you are expected to discuss two concepts in detail backed up by relevant reference to content to answer the task fully in both a) and b). This would mean spending about ten minutes on each section.

Planning your answers briefly might help you ensure you stay relevant and manage to answer all sections of the paper as fully as you can. A quick mind map or bullet pointed list will help you organise your ideas and remember what you intend to write.

 **DON'T FORGET**

Knowing about a number of key aspects for a range of texts will help you ensure you can answer any questions relevantly.

 THINGS TO DO AND THINK ABOUT

1. Make a mind map for each of your texts. Have a section for each key aspect and note down key techniques or concepts and back up each point with specific evidence. This will be a valuable revision tool.

2. Practise exam answers for different texts by using the past papers. This will help you work out how long you take to write each section which will mean you know how to manage your timing.

3. Work with a friend and both attempt an answer. Swap your answers and see if you can apply the mark scheme. Give your friend some tips and see what advice they have for you.

ASSESSMENT

EXTERNAL ASSESSMENT 2

MORE SAMPLE QUESTIONS

At every opportunity, it is advisable to integrate your written answer with at least one other key aspect of media. So, when writing about audience reactions in (a) on the previous pages, for example, it would be good to mention representations, and/or narrative.

The more that you practice analysing texts and using the key aspects, the more it will become clear that they are integrated. Doing this will allow the answer to gain insight, which is required to access the upper level of marks.

For example, if the question were:

1. The ways in which categories are used in the construction of media content can be influenced by society and/or institutional factors.

    Analyse how this statement applies to media content you have studied. In your response you should:

    (a) Analyse the ways in which categories have been used in the construction of the media content. (10)

Then an answer may well start like this:

> The Horror genre can easily be seen through the content of the episodes. For example, in 'Hush', the main villains are the Gentlemen, who are supernatural monsters who steal everyone's voices and start collecting jars of hearts. There are also other supernatural creatures such as vampires, werewolves and demons. This is a common stereotypical convention of horror. There is also lots of fighting and gore, which is part of horror, although this is frequently implied or not lingered on in order to maintain a lower certification. The episode also uses 'horror' camera tricks, such as the **jump scare** when the monster appears suddenly at the window making the character and the audience jump. Music is used effectively with spooky singing of a nursery rhyme in the opening sequence to unsettling creepy sounds that are low and slow, building to a climax, to help build tension. Finally, much of the episode takes place at night so the lighting is often shadowy and creepy.
>
> Another genre that BtVS uses effectively is teen drama. The characters are all teenagers/young adults who experience school and college as well as having to fight the forces of darkness. Buffy, herself, tries to be herself and find out her true identity, which is frequently part of teen drama. She dresses appropriately for her age and is focused on her looks and romance like a typical girl. Her other friends focus on the ups and downs of growing up and finding their place too. Willow explores her sexuality alongside her witchcraft and Xander deals with living in his parents' basement and not attending college like his friends.

Discussion of the conventions of genre lead into a discussion of language features and the representations that they create.

Over the course of the year your assessor should allow you to access or experience a range of texts. In the external exam, you may refer to as many or as few of these texts as you choose. However, it is recommended that you refer to more than just one in the course of the exam.

As part of your revision, you should list the key aspects that you are most comfortable discussing from each text that you have studied. This will allow you to choose the most effective responses to the exam questions.

contd

Assessment: External assessment 2

For example, where a question has been phrased to ask about society:

1. The society in which media content has been created can significantly impact on the construction of a media text in terms of the key aspects of media content.

   Analyse how this statement applies to media content you have studied. In your response you should:

   (a) give detailed information on the various aspects of society that influenced the media content. (10)

... then you need to have examples and content to talk about – and not every text will give you enough depth of information.

An example of how to start to handle this question can be seen below.

KKK: The Fight for White Supremacy is a BBC Three documentary from 2015. It follows Dan Murdoch as he shadows a KKK group and finds out about their lives, their views and the world of the modern KKK in South Carolina.

The film starts with a **montage** that links archive and historical footage with similar modern-day events. This aims to show that the KKK is a well-established group and that racist behaviour has been ongoing in the area for a long time. This is made explicit when a shocking image of a child and adult dressed in matching KKK outfits is shown. This underlines that the society in which the film has been made has a long history of racism and KKK membership, passed from father to son. The film is set in South Carolina, which was part of the breakaway Confederate states during the US Civil War, which was mainly fought because of slavery. It is historically part of the 'Deep South', which is known for its racist attitudes.

Another part of Society that influenced the making of the documentary was the fact that there had been a recent rise in protests and violence associated with police brutality against Black communities. Police had shot a number of young Black men in what were seen as dubious circumstances and there had been significant protests, increased tension and even rioting. During the making of the documentary, a KKK member shot nine Black people and there were protests that the documentary maker attended and included it in the film.

Politically, there are also Society underpinnings to the text. Barack Obama had been elected as the first Black president of the USA. This had proved controversial for racists as they could not reconcile their attitudes with their overt associated jingoistic attitudes. There were a number of conspiracy theories surrounding Obama, including the fact he was not actually born in the USA. One key proponent of this was Donald Trump who succeeded Obama as President. His election campaign fed on racist attitudes and promoted the acceptability of prejudice.

DON'T FORGET

Not only does the SQA website keeps the last three years of exam papers, but also *marking instructions*. This allows you a chance to practice the questions, and also see the marking scheme and see what is actually required of you.

THINGS TO DO AND THINK ABOUT

Get hold of a piece of paper and four different colours of pen/coloured pencil/thin highlighter.

Create a table listing the texts that you have studied. Use the same colour for each of the titles.

Using a second colour, add to the table the key aspects of media literacy that you can comfortably discuss alongside each text.

With a third colour, add in detailed descriptions of scenes where those key aspects can be best shown.

Finally, with a fourth colour, add in the meaning behind the key aspect to which you are referring.

| Dark Knight (Christopher Nolan Dir; Christian Bale, Heath Ledger) | Narrative – Binary Opposition. | In the scene where the Joker has been arrested and is in an interrogation room, Batman appears out of the shadows behind the Joker. For one moment, they are in line – the hero standing behind the villain. | Batman is above the Joker. This represents his moral standing; Batman is moral whereas the Joker is, at best, amoral. It is this morality that is the very thing that the Joker is trying to take away from Batman. |

45

Assessment

EXTERNAL ASSESSMENT 3

ONLINE

Remember – the SQA website (www.sqa.org.uk) has up to the last three years' worth of past papers. These are not locked documents, and are available on the public website. However, Question 3 is brand new for the 2019 diet of exams, therefore you will need to look at the www.understandingstandards.org.uk/Subjects/Media website for exemplar material.

Question 3

Question 3 is commonly referred to as 'the unseen analysis' as it requires you to choose between a pair of film posters, a pair of magazine covers and a pair of print adverts (which you have not seen before the exam) and analyse them.

The question (below) will not change from year to year; the texts chosen will.

> Compare the similarities and differences between the two media texts you have chosen. You need to refer to both texts, make five clear and detailed points of analysis and mention at least two key aspects as evidence.

What is being assessed here is your ability to analyse a text and make connections to another text of a similar genre or form. Straightforward analysis and comparison.

It is important to see that there are a couple of important things that arise from the question that might get missed in the exam rush.

First, *you must make reference to both texts*. If you focus on only one of the pair that you choose then you are limiting yourself to a maximum of 4 marks. Look for similarities and/or differences in the language codes or representations. Discuss how the texts reach different audiences or fulfil similar genre conventions. This does not have to be within the same paragraph; there is no reason why a paragraph on the first text shouldn't be followed by a paragraph on the second: as long as both texts are analysed and some link is made between them.

Second, *in your answer you must make at least five developed points*. Fewer than five points and the marks fall away. Nominally, there are 45 minutes to complete this section (as there are for each of Question 1 and 2) so there is plenty of time to analyse the texts and plan a response. Making that response 'developed' means that the answer has links to the breadth and depth of the analysis. For example, an answer that links the language codes to a break in stereotypical representations would be developed, whereas an answer that merely recounts the language codes would not be.

Starting off

Although you need to make reference to both texts, it is important that you analyse the texts well in the first place.

contd

In this example, some questions have been asked that should prompt your thinking in the exam.

Some questions to ask:

Audience: To which audience does this appeal? Think about age and gender and how you know this.
Institution: Where is the company logo? Is there a particular 'house' style this this company uses?
Society: Is this tied to some point in history (social, political)? Does it fit in with a particular movement or style?
Representation: What is being shown? What is the image of and how is it being depicted?
Language: What colour coding has been used? What does the font/do the fonts suggest? How does the layout show the product?
Categories: How does it achieve the purpose? Is there a clear genre?
Narrative: Is there a narrative structure? – Binary Opposition? A hero on a quest?

Once you have analysed the texts, you should be in a strong position to see where the similarities and the differences are.

In the example below, developed links are made between the language codes and the representations that they are making.

'The first poster depicts a stormy night, with dark clouds and fork-lightning hitting the city. This would stereotypically depict a disaster film, where a city is being destroyed by natural forces. The dark smoke overwhelming the city suggests that there is no hope. However, the bright light on the right-hand side of the poster suggests that dawn is coming. Dawn traditionally symbolises new hope and the chance of survival.

The second poster also involves dark smoke dominating the scene. However, the red lighting gives a much more demonic effect. Rather than a natural disaster, this would appear supernatural or man-made. There is no hope of dawn, only a blood-red mist through which survivors must live …'

THINGS TO DO AND THINK ABOUT

Select two film posters, magazine covers or print adverts from a magazine that you have handy. If possible, select them from similar genres or general themes (perfume adverts, for instance).

Practice analysing each text separately, asking the questions listed above and any others that come to mind (lighting? camera angle? stereotypes?).

Write the answers down.

Now, go through the answers and see where there are links – colours being used the same way, a stereotype that would appeal to an audience, a narrative structure that is shared and so forth.

ROLE OF THE MEDIA

OVERVIEW

HOW TO ANALYSE THE MEDIA

One of the ways to analyse the media is to look at the role it plays in the wider society. You will be expected to be able to discuss the role of the media in terms of how it:

- meets needs (for example, information, education, entertainment)
- influences behaviour and attitudes (either intentionally or unintentionally)
- achieves particular purposes (for example, profit, promotion, public service).

Your teacher may introduce you to a number of theories and concepts to help you analyse the different roles of the media.

One key idea that runs throughout the idea of Role is the idea of power – who has the power in the media and how do they use it? In the past, the media would present a particular view of the world that would be disseminated to the audience. This was often used to reinforce desired values and ideas by the people who controlled the media and censor unwanted information. One example of this is that the government used D-notices to ban certain stories from being published, such as the affair between the Prince of Wales and Wallis Simpson in the 1930s. Newer technology offers the chance to interact more and select where information comes from. It is not hierarchical or one-directional but interactive and multi-directional. Social media, for example, allows people to share information, images and videos from ongoing incidents instantly.

This ties in with three common perspectives on the media: traditionalist, capitalist and public service.

TRADITIONAL, CAPITALIST AND PUBLIC SERVICE PERSPECTIVES

The traditionalist perspective states that the media should uphold traditional values, such as law and order and 'family values'. It also suggests that the media can have a harmful effect on society and needs to be censored in respect of sex and violence. This is quite a conservative point of view.

The capitalist perspective states that the media have responsibility to owners and shareholders and can use a free market to deliver wealth to owners, while offering democracy and diversity to consumers. It suggests that public service media should be privatised (for example, universal BBC licence should be replaced by subscription) and that media should be deregulated. Capitalists also believe there should be no barriers to concentrated media ownership. This viewpoint is often categorised as neoliberal.

The public service perspective suggests that the media have a democratic responsibility towards society and must fulfil social functions of transmission of information, equal access and creation of a public forum for different viewpoints. It also suggests that the media collectively should represent diverse social groups and reflect diversity through a range of viewpoints and should allow access to diverse social groups. Another important idea is that the media should be independent from interference from business and government and should apply self-regulation with regard to content and conduct. Media markets should be regulated to prevent domination by a single or a few large corporations. Society is entitled to high standards and intervention justifiable if the media fail to meet these standards. This is seen as quite a liberal point of view.

Role of the Media: Overview

OTHER USES FOR AUDIENCE THEORIES

Audience theories can also be used to think about the way the role of the media works. In the past, the Effect model was very popular. It came from the US and suggested a 'hypodermic needle effect' of media content affecting passive users who just accepted what they were being shown without thinking. This was replaced by a uses and gratifications model at the other end of the scale. This suggested that users take different gratification or pleasure from the media they consume. Nowadays, the main trend is for studying **discourse**, meaning and power. This looks at how texts are encoded and how the audience decodes these, whether they accept the preferred meaning of the texts or whether they approach it with a negotiated, differential or oppositional reading.

The media also plays an important role in establishing national identity. Jürgen Habermas, a German philosopher and sociologist, suggested that the media provides a public space for discussion and opinion and engages people in society and its development. He claims that the media has a role in stimulating and informing debate, representing public opinion, acting as an inclusive discussion forum and nurturing public belonging and community. The dominant forms of media have successfully done this in the past through print, then radio, then TV. However, with the ways in which we consume media splintering further and further, there is an argument that this is no longer true.

DON'T FORGET

You need to be able to answer on any of the roles specified as you do not know what will come up in the exam.

IMPERIALISM AND GLOBALISATION

Another two concepts associated with the role of the media are cultural imperialism and **globalisation**. These can be viewed as a positive development – building a *global village*, the idea that shared media builds connections across the world, linking us – and more negatively as *cultural imperialism* – where powerful capitalist interests in wealthy countries dominate poorer countries to maximise profit and minimise costs, aiming to sell cultural products around the world to a huge market. It is true that many media products are now produced with a global market in mind. However, this lack of locally specific difference forces poorer countries to rely on cheap imports rather than producing their own, resulting in homogenisation (everything being the same). Media companies want to maintain their freedom to operate and make profit, so they use their products to spread a **dominant ideology** that makes capitalism and consumerism natural and inevitable. The ability to access imagery, sounds, music, commerce and ideas from anywhere in the world seems attractive but the idea of some monolithic global culture seems less pleasant.

These are just some of the concepts and ideas that you might want to consider as you think about the different roles of the media. Depending on the texts you study, you might choose to incorporate some of them or totally ignore them. However, the ideas of power and who has it underpins many of the examples in the next few pages.

 THINGS TO DO AND THINK ABOUT

Look at a selection of newspaper front pages. What ideas are they promoting? What do they want you to do or to think? Do they have any stories in common? How have they presented these stories?

Do some research into who owns these newspapers. What values or ideology do these owners have? How can you see this in your selection of newspaper front pages?

 ONLINE TEST

Test your knowledge of the Role of the Media paper at www.brightredbooks.net/subjects

ROLE OF THE MEDIA

MEETING AUDIENCE NEEDS

Under meeting needs, you are asked to think about entertainment, education and information.

WHAT DO I GET OUT OF IT?

One popular console-based game is the *Call of Duty* series. This is a first-person shooting game, which has gone through several iterations. According to statistics, more than 50 million people are registered online players of at least one of the series.

Players will happily stay up through the night playing games with other online users (from other countries) because there are feelings of community: of shared values and interests. For some, often parents, it is difficult to understand why such a community cannot be found with 'real' friends, but the gameplay, addictive as adolescents find it, and the shared camaraderie of battle remain intensely appealing. For the target audience – teenagers and adolescents – the need to meet with like-minded people and share experiences is the key to the role that the game plays.

A similar story, in terms of shared values and interests, applies to social media sites. The last decade has seen a huge growth in social media sites that allow users to share their lives with friends online. Without doubt, Facebook has been the outstanding app, offering users the ability to post photos, videos, memes, messages and instant messages, as well as play online games. More recently, Twitter and Instagram have become major forces. Twitter's limitation of 140 characters leads to short, often enigmatic, messages or photos that inspire conversation and interaction with 'followers' (as friends are known in the tweeting world).

Social media and online gaming fulfil an audience need for community and acceptance. This is what the audience get out of the media texts, and that is what keeps them engaging with the texts.

A sense of community and shared values is a significant part of what audiences get from media texts. Yet, there is more.

NOT JUST ONLINE ...

Every year, millions of people visit art galleries and museums across the world (approximately 10.2 million people visited the Louvre in 2018). The texts on exhibit in these places fulfil an audience need for curiosity. Audiences want to engage with great works of art and they either sympathise with them and the feelings of the artist involved, or they disagree.

Notice that the *purpose* for which the text was produced may differ from the *role* it may play in society. It is highly likely that da Vinci painted *Mona Lisa* to receive some kind of payment or preference (the profit purpose at work again). However, the role it plays in today's society is to allow the audience to wonder at the genius that produced it and to serve as an inspiration. As one artist commented: '*art is a vehicle for the transmission of ideas through form*', and that fulfils the audience's need to see it up close.

EDUCATE, ENTERTAIN, INFORM ...

Over and above meeting the psychological needs of audiences, texts can also educate, entertain or inform an audience.

Throughout the history of mass media, audiences have changed from being passive (believing whatever they see or hear), have gone through a phase of being very active (questioning everything within a text) and may have cycled back round to passivity again (where many are happy to pass on media information without questioning or thinking).

On 30 October 1938, there was a radio broadcast in New York that has become famous (or infamous). It started as something that had the purpose of entertaining the audience. It was a Halloween story about an alien invasion.

However, for some of the audience, the role it took was something more serious. Orson Welles's dramatisation of H. G. Wells's *The War of the Worlds* was based on news reports. It appears that some of the audience did not hear the start of the programme, announcing that it was a radio drama, but rather picked up 'news' reports about a Martian invasion of Earth. It may sound far-fetched, but it is the same time period that Joseph Goebbels was spreading propaganda unhindered throughout Nazi Germany. A passive audience accepts a passive role for media.

© 2018 Pat Bian

The growth of social media, with the community that it creates, has meant that many of the features of that passivity have returned. The trust that is placed in the community means that anything that is shared can be trusted and re-shared without an investigation or questioning.

Newspapers can be seen as firmly overlapping all three needs of information, entertainment and education. Most newspapers blend the need to provide information and educate their readers about issues, politics and current affairs with entertaining articles on lifestyle, sports and culture. Some newspapers focus more on the entertainment end of the spectrum, printing stories about celebrities and scandals. This is where they are often open to criticism and questions about whether they are problematic.

THINGS TO DO AND THINK ABOUT

Watch an advert on television or a documentary and ask, 'What is the audience getting out of this?' Is it fulfilling a need to belong, or a need to learn something new? Is it seeking to create a community (where only certain people belong – like a bingo group or a special holiday-booking website)?

ONLINE

Watch the War of the Worlds Panic Documentary at our Digital Zone www.brightredbooks.net/subjects

DON'T FORGET

Over time, the needs that a text meets for the audience might change. Something entertaining in the past may now be seen as informing the audience about that time period.

ONLINE TEST

Test your knowledge of meeting audience needs at www.brightredbooks.net/subjects

ROLE OF THE MEDIA

MEETING PURPOSES OF INSTITUTIONS

There are three purposes behind institutions creating a media text that are identified by the SQA. They will want to create profit, promote a service or brand or they will seek to achieve a public service. The texts you study will probably fit into one of these three areas, if not overlap them.

ONLINE

Go on to our Digital Zone to find out more about the dictionary definition of public service.

PUBLIC SERVICE

The Collins dictionary defines public service as being *'something such as health care, transport, or the removal of waste which is organized by the government or an official body in order to benefit all the people in a particular society or community'*.

When it comes to public service in media, most often, it means a documentary or a government public information that promotes such services.

PUBLIC INFORMATION FILM

This much-copied poster was originally created by the British government in 1938. It was designed to be published in the event of a Nazi invasion of the British Isles. It is an example of a public service media text. In the event of an invasion, the government's instructions to the people of the country was to keep calm and carry on as normal. There is no other reason for the text to exist other than to communicate information to the target audience.

Once in a while, a commercial company will sneak public service into an advert so that it combines with their need for profit. One example of this is Dove's 'Real Beauty' campaign. While promoting Dove's hygiene products, the campaign has also attempted to highlight the inequalities (and hypocrisy) of the beauty industry and the way in which it treats women.

VIDEO LINK

One of the more famous videos showing this campaign and what it sought to do can be found at www.brightredbooks.net/subjects

News organisations will often say that they are providing a public service, giving information in an impartial, truthful and accurate way. However, there are a number of problems with this. News organisations have editors who select what is considered to be news and what is not; they act as 'gatekeepers'. Equally, the news does not always present a balanced, truthful reflection of the world. The Independent Press Standards Organisation currently regulates the UK press and can uphold complaints.

PROMOTING A BRAND OR SERVICE

The most obvious manner in which a media text promotes a brand or service is through advertising – in all its forms from films though billboards and even including the Google ads that pop up throughout our use of the Internet.

VIDEO LINK

Watch the John Lewis advert in question at www.brightredbooks.net/subjects

In the UK, companies vie to see who will have the most powerful or popular Christmas advert. For the last few years, the department store John Lewis has dominated this unofficial competition. With each advert, the institution that is John Lewis is promoting itself and the products it sells. This is especially true of the 2014 advert, 'Monty the Penguin'. Everything shown in the advert: the boy's pyjamas, the bed clothes, sports equipment, household items ... *and the penguin* ... all are or were available at John Lewis stores. By showing the advert, the products of the store are being promoted.

Social media sites can also be used to promote brands and products. The ways in which different social media platforms appeal to different audiences is something that is a major part of any marketing campaign. An interesting example of this can be seen in the different ways the Colorado Avalanche ice hockey team uses their different social media

contd

Role of the Media: Meeting purposes of institutions

channels cleverly to promote their brand. Their social media, regardless of network, is seeking to raise awareness of their brand. They have several different audiences that they need to attract. Stereotypical ice hockey fans need to be catered to. The team website, Facebook and YouTube channel focus on these traditional, stereotypical fans, with a focus on games and scores. On the other hand, the social media team is also trying to broaden and diversify the fanbase, aiming towards younger fans through Snapchat and Twitter and to women through Instagram and Tumblr.

By encouraging a wider fanbase, the social media team achieves the entire purpose behind the sports team: profit. Fans are needed to buy tickets (preferably season tickets) and show up to games. They are also needed to watch games on screens, on television or through the various official apps available. This allows the team to gain more money from television rights. Dedicated fans will also purchase merchandise, from replica jerseys to mugs to toys. More views will also attract more sponsorship of specific elements, for example, the Avalanche 360 YouTube channel, which will also mean more money funnelling into the team.

ONLINE

Go to our Digital Zone at www.brightredbooks.net/subjects for more links to investigate this topic!

PROFIT

Companies need to make profit in order to survive. The adverts that have been mentioned – Dove and John Lewis – also have, at their heart, the drive for profit. Arguably every media product, with the possible exception of some artwork, and government-funded information texts, has profit as its core motive and role. It exists to create profit for the institution behind it.

What needs to be established, however, in any text, is what elements of the text will appeal to a target audience and so create the profit.

Dove's 'Real Beauty' campaign appeals to women through the portrayal of 'normal' women as opposed to models. It appeals to women who have lumps and bumps and who do not conform to society's stereotypical viewpoint of what beauty is. Showing a size 12 model, rather than a size 6 model, is appealing and will encourage those women to purchase Dove products – increasing profit.

By showing items that can be bought in John Lewis stores, the institution is encouraging the watching public to see something that they like/would want. The families portrayed in the adverts are aspirational – they are living a lifestyle that others may want. By shopping at John Lewis (and providing the company with profit), customers will feel that they can achieve that lifestyle.

Newspapers are also mainly aiming to make a profit for their owners and shareholders. This might be why they choose the stories they do – focusing on **celebrity** gossip or particular scandalous images to sell more papers rather than select more boring but worthy news items. Sometimes this causes problems, when newspapers choose to make up stories that sound entertaining or undermine serious stories with comedic pun-laden headlines.

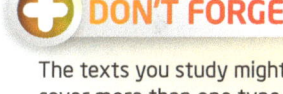

DON'T FORGET

The texts you study might cover more than one type of purpose.

 THINGS TO DO AND THINK ABOUT

Visit a range of news organisation's websites. Identify which sections are aiming to give information and which ones are aiming to entertain. What do you notice about the use of images? What about the use of journalists' names?

ONLINE TEST

Test your knowledge of meeting the purposes of institutions at www.brightredbooks.net/subjects

ROLE OF THE MEDIA

INFLUENCING BEHAVIOUR

DOING IT ON PURPOSE

During the Edinburgh Festival, it is almost impossible to walk down a street without being handed a flyer. These are pieces of paper, often small, which have been designed to advertise a show or performance that is being put on during the festival. The information on the sheet will include the title, creator, date, time and venue of the performance; often a promotional shot from the event; and some reviews from newspapers.

These flyers are designed to influence the behaviour of those who receive them – this is the role that they play. Those who are within the target audience will take note of the performance and will be attracted by the picture or the play, and will buy tickets and attend: their behaviour will have been influenced by the flyer.

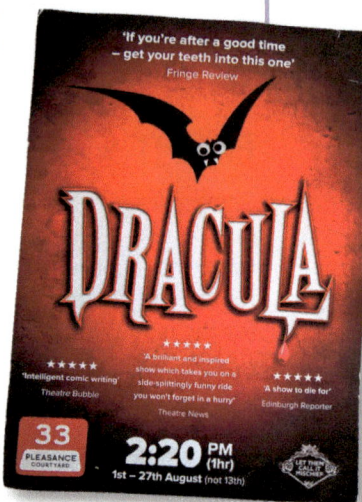

Earlier in the Role of Media section, we looked at adverts. These are, clearly, also designed to influence the behaviour. John Lewis's Christmas adverts are designed to influence the behaviour of those who watch. The adverts pull on the emotions of the audience, often appealing to sentimentality as children or animals are shown to be cute or selfless.

The key thing with influencing behaviour is the method – appealing to emotions such as fear. Adverts on television and flyers in the street, while possibly powerful, are not dangerous enough to influence a whole society. Government films are the next level up.

VIDEO LINK

Check out the government advert at www.brightredbooks.net/subjects

In response to the death rate on train tracks in Melbourne, Australia, the metro company created the animated series *Dumb Ways to Die*. Using dark humour and a very catchy song, the animations highlight to the audience the dangers of acting foolishly around the rail network. The audience is influenced by the absurdity of the animation (which likens playing on the railway track to using your private parts for piranha bait). The silliness of the 'dumb ways to die' serves to highlight the silliness of playing near a railway, and behaviour is influenced accordingly.

In the 1980s, a threat was detected from a new disease: acquired immune deficiency syndrome (AIDS). The PIF noted here was issued by the British government in order to raise awareness of the disease and influence the behaviour of the audience.

It was released nationally and avoids stating any particular target audience during the voice-over. Everyone is included in the message – and the message is based on fear. Through oppressive images – volcanoes, dark stone – heavy voice-over and the final image of a tombstone, the government sought to put fear into the hearts of the audience and scare them into changing their behaviour.

It is worth looking at one more example. What if a government does not want to influence its citizens for good?

Historically, few governments have managed to create such a barrage of propaganda designed to influence the behaviour of their people more than the Nazi government of Germany from 1933 until 1945.

Through the use of fear and long-held emotional beliefs regarding the Jewish people, Hitler and his government brought many millions of people to believe that the racist policies of the National Socialist Party were correct. The posters used grotesque, cartoon depictions of Jews, coupled with stylised, ideal depictions of the 'Master Race'. The population of Germany – the audience – was to be influenced against the Jews and so not care or act when the government 'sorted the problem'.

contd

Role of the Media: Influencing behaviour

Detection of this type of influence is not, sadly, confined to history. As the 21st century dawned, it was clear that six companies effectively govern all the news and media in the world. One of these is semi-British (21st Century Fox); the rest are American.

In recent years, the UK has gone through one Independence Referendum in Scotland in 2014, along with a referendum to decide to leave the European Union in 2016. The United States has elected a new President in 2016 – the first to have no political background whatsoever.

All three of these campaigns were fought through the use of multi-media. All three of these campaigns fought hard to influence the behaviour of the audiences, through news channels, posters and adverts. All three campaigns used the same methods that are used in theatre flyers and Christmas adverts: strong emotions and images, along with the fear tactics used by governments.

 ONLINE

Go to our Digital Zone at www.brightredbooks.net/subjects for more links to investigate this topic!

INTENTIONAL OR UNINTENTIONAL?

The messages that media texts send to audiences are mainly intended. However, sometimes the texts reinforce attitudes and behaviours unintentionally.

One of the biggest problems with advertising is the way in which they reinforce gender stereotypes. Children's advertising already begins to reinforce particular ideas about gender. Toys are split by gender very clearly, with certain products aimed at boys and others at girls. The toys aimed at boys tend to be technology based, suggesting that boys are more suited to technology, computers and science, technology, engineering and mathematics (STEM) fields whereas girls are excluded. Girls face a similar narrow selection of toys. Most girl-centred toys seem focused on caring and appearance. These adverts reinforce the idea that women are weak and men are strong. It also limits girls to either a nurturing role or makes them believe that appearance is all that matters. Boys are limited as well. They are forced into an attitude of strength and power and not shown as being permitted to like nurturing and caring. This narrowing of attitudes creates a sexist society where male and female roles are strictly delineated. Adult advertising also reinforces this delineation. The majority of adverts for technology are male-focused whereas whereas a similar majority of adverts for domestic products were female orientated.

 **DON'T FORGET**

Purpose will often help you work out what behaviour or attitude a text is aiming to influence. Representation is also very important here.

A similar criticism of gender stereotype reinforcement is often levelled at Disney and its princess films in particular. Disney princesses are said to be focused on beauty and romance, waiting for a prince to come save them. Disney is challenging this portrayal of women through its more recent Disney princesses, such as Elsa and Anna from *Frozen*, who save each other through their sisterly bond and Moana, where the titular lead character has no romantic storyline and drives the entire film. Disney's Dream Big, Princess advertising also explicitly linked the princesses to a more feminist portrayal of gender.

THINGS TO DO AND THINK ABOUT

Watch an episode of a current television programme you enjoy. What messages about behaviour and attitudes are being suggested to the audience? Think about gender, age, race, education level and so forth. Look at a film or programme made in the past. How do the messages it sends about behaviour or attitudes differ from ones in the present day?

 ONLINE TEST

Test your knowledge of influencing behaviour at www.brightredbooks.net/subjects

ROLE OF THE MEDIA

ASSESSMENT

THE ROLE OF THE MEDIA PAPER

The Role of the Media paper is worth 20 marks (15% of your grade) and you are allowed an hour to answer. Advice from the SQA is that you answer on different texts and examples from Paper 1. The other key advice from the Course Report is that candidates who answered on a range of texts were more successful than candidates who answered on one to exemplify their points, arguments or opinions.

The SQA wants a clear line of argument answering the question and showing a knowledge of a range of issues, commenting critically or giving personal opinions. This should be solidly backed up by referring to examples from the text. Integrating parts a) and b) generally seemed to offer more success than trying to answer the two sections separately. Answers that only give information about how texts have been created to meet the role of the media without commenting or giving opinions were not able to achieve a great many marks, as with answers that focused on one side of the argument only. You are required to respond to the unknown task set in the exam rather than regurgitate a learned answer.

TIPS

- *Read* the question carefully. It should suggest which evidence/elements to include.
- *Plan* your answer – you have an hour to ensure you know what you are going to say.
- *Link* everything back to the question.
- Use the *PEE* structure – Point/Evidence/Explanation – to help you develop ideas in detail.
- Your answer does not need to be an *essay*. It can be developed *bullet points*. Use *headings* to help you organise.

Planning your answer

This is the style of question: 'The media is often accused of being problematic, for example, breaking the law or invading privacy. In response, the media claims it is just meeting the requirements or needs of its audiences.'

Thinking through what you want to write is a good way to make sure you organise your thoughts and construct a line of argument. Creating a table might be a quick way of doing this. This candidate is answering on the popular press.

Meeting needs for	Problematic
Providing information in the public interest	Invading privacy
Entertaining stories	Made up stories, lies, disrespectful
Creating sense of national identity	Promoting ideology of owner

A mind map might also help you think about what to write.

Writing your answer

You should start with an introduction clearly outlining your line of thought. Often rewriting the question can help here.

'Every media content has been made to achieve a particular purpose, ranging from clearly apparent to more elusive. There may also be more than one purpose.'

contd

Role of the Media: Assessment

Example:

Advertising is media content that has been constructed to meet the particular purpose of selling a product. This is its main obvious purpose, but advertising also serves to reinforce the status quo and capitalistic ideology.

You can present your ideas however you like. A simple formula like Point–Evidence–Explanation will help you fulfil all the marking criteria. This example integrates both ideas and examples to create a straightforward but detailed answer.

Example:

Point – Advertising often reinforces gender stereotypes, influencing behaviour and attitudes.

Evidence – An example of this would be Beats Headphones. The adverts for these tend to depict sportsmen, particularly American ones, thereby linking technology with sport, another stereotypical male interest. The Hear What You Want advert takes this a step further by using a song with the lyrics 'I'm the man', again reinforcing the idea that technology use is integral to masculinity. Domestic products such as cleaning products are stereotypically focused on women. An example of this is the Flash A-Ha Dog advert where the female houseowner is shown to be pleased that she has managed to clean up all the mud with the use of Flash to make her house very clean.

Explanation – This reinforces the stereotype that men are interested in technology and women are only seen in domestic settings as housewives and caretakers. The counter-argument here is that men spend money on technology whereas women are responsible for most grocery and household shopping so therefore the adverts should be aimed at them. However, it does seem like a circular argument as one reinforces the other.

Because you are writing an argument, signal which words are important to show where you are comparing and contrasting. It helps your marker see where your line of thought is progressing. You would often use these at the start of new paragraphs and sections.

- On one hand
- On the other hand
- However
- In contrast
- In addition

One requirement of the Role of the Media paper is the need to draw a conclusion. This should come naturally from your line of argument. A conclusion sums up your points very briefly and gives an answer to the question.

Example:

In conclusion, there are arguments on both sides for the UK popular press being out-of-control and problematic. It is important that the newspaper's audience are informed and entertained in order to meet their needs, but the means used to gain these stories must also be carefully and sensitively monitored. Illegal and immoral means of gaining a story must be investigated, independently, and journalists should be held to their ethical code.

 **DON'T FORGET**

You must answer the question. You must be able to use your knowledge to build a relevant argument.

 THINGS TO DO AND THINK ABOUT

Apply this to your own knowledge. Try to plan out an answer for each of the three Role of the Media elements. How do your texts meet needs, achieve purposes or influence behaviour or attitudes?

 **ONLINE TEST**

Test your knowledge of the Role of the Media paper at www.brightredbooks.net/subjects

ROLE OF THE MEDIA

ASSESSMENT — EXAMPLE

All media content can be described as having been constructed to meet a particular purpose. In some content there may be one, obvious purpose; in other content there may be several purposes, some quite subtle.

SAMPLE STUDENT ANSWER

Advertising is media content that has been constructed to meet the particular purpose of selling a product. This is its main obvious purpose, but advertising also serves to reinforce the status quo and capitalistic ideology.

In order to sell a product, modern advertisers are looking to create a 'market' of loyal purchasers. One key way of doing this is through the development of a brand. Branding establishes a personality for a product or range of products. One way of doing this is through linked advertising. Lynx is a good example of this. Their adverts are known for appealing to the 'ordinary' bloke and sell the idea that women will be attracted to you if you use this product. Some adverts choose to exaggerate this (the Chocolate man advert) whereas the more recent ones choose to do this through selling the idea of being an individual and challenging stereotypes. Interestingly, they include a range of depictions of masculinity with homosexuality and disability represented. The men in the advert are still overwhelmingly young and attractive and the message of 'getting the girl' is still central. Lynx also sponsor the panda-mating programme at Edinburgh Zoo, linked to their idea of attractiveness being important and a campaign called 'Ditch the Label' that promotes individuality and anti-bullying. Combined, these all establish Lynx as a brand that has a strong identity that consumers can identify with and therefore become loyal customers, selecting the brand name over other similar products.

Often a product will attempt to establish a Unique Selling Point (USP) to persuade customers that their product is the one that should be purchased. In reality, there is a limited amount of difference between products. A key example of this would be Pepsi versus Coca-Cola where the brands claim to be very different, yet they are basically the same. Pepsi tends to pursue celebrity endorsement and link itself with music whereas Coca-Cola portrays 'ordinary' consumers and sponsors sporting events such as the Football World Cup and the Olympics. Coca-Cola's USP is linked to bringing people together (Enjoy a coke with ... being a recent campaign) whereas Pepsi seems to be about glamour.

One of the main ways in which advertising supports the idea of capitalism is through the idea that having 'stuff' means you are happy. Another way of thinking about this would be to see that success is equivalent to wealth. An example of this would be the modern adverts for Old Spice, the men's grooming product. Here the man shows that in order to attract a woman, you have to have diamonds, a yacht, tickets to 'that thing she likes'. While this is demeaning for women, there is the very clear message that having 'stuff' is good. This materialism also reinforces envy and hedonism – the idea that you are the only person who matters.

Stereotyping in advertising is used to reinforce the status quo as well. Gender roles are often reinforced through advertising. It begins early, with adverts aimed at children. Toys are coded into boys and girls, with boys' toys including technology, Lego and building things. These often include the colour blue, upbeat and dramatic music and male voice-overs. Lego is a good example of this, with all the depicted characters being male. This suggests that boys are creative and like to build things. In opposition, many toy adverts aimed at girls promote appearance and caring, such as the Puppy in My Pocket adverts, which is mainly in pastel pinks and purples. The dogs are there to be looked after and can also form accessories, reinforcing the idea that looks are what matters.

contd

Adult advertising is also reliant on gender stereotyping. 70 per cent of adverts for technology are aimed at men and 66 per cent of domestic product advertising is aimed at women. Car advertising tends to be explicitly male. For example, the recent range of Jaguar adverts use male celebrities such as Tom Hiddleston and Sir Ben Kingsley linking to their roles as supervillains. This links men to power and intelligence. Domestic products such as Flash tend to be shown being used by women only, selling the idea that women's place is in the home. The counter-argument to this is that women are responsible for home shopping and men for technology. But it would appear that this is a circular argument as one reinforces the other.

Another type of stereotyping that reinforces the status quo is that of national stereotyping. This creates a narrow image of other countries as well as perhaps reinforcing a certain narrow view of ourselves. It is used as advertising relies on familiarity to engage the viewer but perhaps this familiarity needs to be questioned. A classic example of depicting the 'Other' is the Fry's Turkish Delight advert from the 1980s, which says the product is 'Full of Eastern Promise'. It uses imagery associated with the Middle East, such as sensual women, sheikhs with a headdress and scimitar, sand dunes and snakes. It creates an unrealistic depiction of Turkey that is firmly rooted in the past, reinforcing the idea that people from there are uncivilised, sex-hungry barbarians. It generalises the Arab world as well as underlining the idea that 'they' are not like 'us'. A more recent example using exactly the same type of stereotyping is the Carphone Warehouse advert starring Keith Lemon, set in Dubai. The men he associates with are all dressed in the stereotypical headdress and clothing much the same as the Fry's advert. He goes to Dubai because it is full of extreme wealth, but it still relies on camels and sand dunes to suggest the location. Again, it is generalised and unrealistic, reinforcing racist stereotypes.

Equally adverts claiming to represent Britishness often rely on the UKIP vision of England, with Britain being a monolithic non-diverse culture. The Mars #believe advert is a clear example of this, supporting English football at the Euros 2016 and ignoring the presence of Wales and Northern Ireland. It is actually very distasteful, depicting 'England' supporters crossing the Channel in makeshift boats to France. While the intended reading was to link with Dunkirk or D-Day, it instead creates an association with the refugees drowning in the Mediterranean, fleeing war. It also represents the French as wimps with poodles – a girly dog? – and the English as Knights, Elizabeth I, soldiers in dress uniform and tea ladies, relying on nostalgia for the past and on the notion of strength. The 'invaders' are also predominantly white. Tetley tea also reinforces this through its recent 'Best of British' advert where its animated characters take a trip through Historical Britain to say tea has always been essential. They select Winston Churchill, The Beatles, the 1966 England World Cup victory and so on. The intended reading would be a pride in Britishness, recalling perhaps the opening of the 2012 London Olympics, but instead it limits British to English again, having only one person of colour in the entire advert and reinforcing a nostalgic view of Britain unrelated to the modern country. The products are attempting to use national identity to associate their products with national pride but instead are reinforcing a very narrow, stereotypical view of the country that excludes more than it includes.

Advertising achieves a number of different purposes. Its main one remains selling a product, which it does through creating a brand and using USPs. However, intended or not, advertising also achieves the purpose of reinforcing the status quo, particularly through the use of stereotyping.

DON'T FORGET

You have an hour to answer this paper. You should be able to write in a lot of detail.

THINGS TO DO AND THINK ABOUT

Look at the above example. Identify the different parts of the candidate's answer. Can you find their introduction and conclusion? What are their main points? Can you work out what this student's plan would have looked like?

ONLINE TEST

Test your knowledge of the Role of the Media paper at www.brightredbooks.net/subjects

PRODUCTION

PRODUCTION

RESEARCH, PLANNING, PRODUCTION AND EVALUATION

Half of your course will focus on Production. This is the creation of media content. You will have various resources available to you in your centre and you have to decide how to make best use of them in order to create a product. There are four stages in completing a production:

- Research
- Planning
- Production
- Evaluation

By completing each stage, you will ensure your production meets your creative intentions. These are what you intend your product to be. You also have to take into consideration the purpose you intend it to meet and the target audience.

STIMULUS AND NEGOTIATION

You will be provided with a brief, much as a professional media producer would be given a brief by a client. This will detail a rough set of demands for your product.

There will be something along the lines of an instruction or a stimulus. An instruction could be to make something for a particular purpose, such as an advert or a documentary. Stimuli could be used to suggest ideas – an extract from a book or a news story. You will also be given your target audience and the level of finish expected. At Higher, your level of finish must be a completed product or a completed part of one text (for example, a scene from a longer film or two or three pages from a newspaper or magazine) that uses a range of media codes and conventions.

Example: Sample brief
- The target audience for your product is secondary school pupils.
- Your product should be based on a poem. The poem must be selected by you.
- The purpose of your product is to deepen understanding of a poetry text. It should be a complete product.

This brief allows you to choose what your content is to be, whether it is a magazine, a poster or a film. It gives you quite a specific audience of secondary school pupils but there is still a possibility of negotiating a more specific audience within that – will your content appeal to younger or older pupils? What about gender? The purpose is also quite open, and you could interpret it in a number of different ways. You could choose to go down a non-fiction route and produce a documentary or perhaps do something more artistic and dramatic and make an interpretive short film.

Discussing your ideas with your assessor and negotiating these elements is a key part of media production. They will be able to guide you although they will not be able to tell you what to do. That has to come from your skills and knowledge and what you learn during your production unit.

Individual skills

There are some key skills that you will use in media production. These skills are helpful not just in media during the course but in whatever career you choose to pursue. These are transferable skills.

contd

DON'T FORGET

You need to meet the brief for your product to succeed. Pay close attention to it.

- Creativity is not just having a good imagination. It is being able to think around an idea and come up with lots of different suggestions. Inventiveness is perhaps a better way of thinking about this.
- Problem solving is also important. Instead of giving up when something does not quite go to plan, think about the problem and work out how to change, adapt or even rework it to ensure that the problem does not occur again. Taking time to think about what has happened and persisting will mean you do not fail to complete your product.
- Patience is also essential. Whether it is patience with other people who perhaps do not work as quickly as you do or whether it is with yourself when you realise you do not yet know how something works, you need the ability to stay calm and work through the obstacle.
- Time management is a key part of media production as often deadlines are very short. There is a saying that time is money, which means that the longer something takes, the more expensive it is. While there might not be cost implications during your production, you will have very strict external guidelines set by the SQA that you must meet or you will fail. Planning your time effectively will ensure you do not make a production that does not reflect the best of your ability.

Working in a group

Sometimes your assessor will direct you to work as part of a group and sometimes you will work independently. Working in a group does not mean you can rely on others to complete the bulk of the tasks – you must show evidence of fulfilling all the requirements of the course individually.

Working as part of a group requires a range of skills. You will probably be accustomed to working in a group but some reminders are always useful.

- Communication is vital. You need to not only have the confidence to explain your own ideas but you have to be able to listen to other people. Asking questions to clarify and expand on others' ideas and to get an idea of their feelings is also an important skill. Groups that pay attention to one another's feelings will often be more successful than those who do not.
- Openness is very important. Being able to take on new ideas and listen to others is essential. Getting to know other people in your group allows this openness to be created.
- Respect is a word that we use a lot. It is often something we say we want. You need to demonstrate respect in order to receive it. This includes focusing on being honest, trusting the group and trying to learn from mistakes rather than lingering on assigning blame.
- Supporting one another is a way that groups can help everyone succeed. This is essential in the world of media creation where you are collaborators, not competitors.

THINGS TO DO AND THINK ABOUT

Before you begin your production, evaluate your skills. What do you do well? What do you not know about yet? Where are you going to gain new skills? Who can help?

PRODUCTION

AUDIENCE AND RESEARCH

RESEARCH: AN OVERVIEW

Doing research is a key part of any media producer's job. It is important to understand your audience's needs and expectations. You should also develop an understanding of what sort of problems and controls you might face as part of your production.

Finally, you should look at similar content to find out what kind of techniques it uses. You then need to explain how this research has influenced your planning decisions.

Start with the Brief

Having a clear idea of what the brief requires in terms of audience, content and product, will make research much easier. This is also your starting point for research. You should clearly identify your audience and what you are going to produce. If you are not sure, negotiate with your assessor.

AUDIENCE RESEARCH

The first stage is to identify who your audience is and what their characteristics are. If your audience is everyone, you might not end up having a specific enough product. Equally, if your audience is too narrow, it might be difficult to get enough people to engage with it.

Think about the purpose of your product. Who is likely to need or want it? You should now aim to describe your **demographic**.

Think about:

- Age group
- Gender
- Location
- Income level
- Education level
- Occupation

You might also consider:

- Personality
- Attitudes
- Interests or hobbies
- Behaviour

This will give you a clear idea of what your audience looks like.

The next step is to think about your audience's needs, wants and preferences. Audience analysis will also help you to avoid offending your audience or making your product too simple, or too complex for them to understand.

There are a number of ways you could find out this information, including speaking to your audience, observing them, and 'audience targeting'.

Production: Audience and research

SPEAKING TO YOUR AUDIENCE

You might be able to run a questionnaire or a focus group with your audience in order to find out what they want and what they prefer.

Step 1
Write down the questions you want answers to. Use question words like who/what/where/why/when and how. Aim to ask open questions in a focus group that require an explanation. If you are running a questionnaire, you probably want to limit your questions to more simply answered closed questions.

Step 2
Try out your questions on a volunteer. Use their answers to think about whether your question will get the answer you need. Redraft your questions.

Step 3
Run your research. Questionnaires can gather lots of information quickly, but sometimes people do not like to fill them in. Focus groups require more time, but will result in a deeper understanding of your audience. You also have to make sure you take lots of notes.

Step 4
Analyse your research. Are there any common answers? What information have you learned?

OBSERVATION

Sometimes it will not be appropriate to ask your audience questions directly. Imagine your audience is infants and toddlers! You then need to observe your audience. Equally, your audience might be your peer group. Talking to them and spending time with them, and then thinking about what you have observed might also provide you with valuable research into audience. Another way of observing might be to look at social media and examine what people are saying about products like the one you intend to make.

DON'T FORGET

Be careful to make sure you take lots of notes and write down what you have found out. You will need to demonstrate what you have learned to your assessor.

AUDIENCE TARGETING

Another way to learn about your audience would be to look at content that is already aimed at your audience. Quite often, for example, the audience is inscribed or present in the text. Equally, the producers might have developed the content to include particular sounds or images. Take notes on what is included to appeal to this audience. This could include representation, language, categories or narrative. Use your analysis skills to help you.

You could also find out if similar content has an audience profile already. Magazines often produce media kits for their brands to tell advertisers what their audience looks like, what they like and how much they earn. Commercial television channels and radio stations also often create media kits to entice advertisers. Similarly, public service television channels often explain who they are seeking to target with their commissioning information. This could provide the basis for you to develop your ideas about audience.

ONLINE

Head to www.brightredbooks.net to find a list of websites to help with audience targeting.

 ## THINGS TO DO AND THINK ABOUT

It is important that you put audience at the core of your product. You must think carefully about their needs, wants and preferences as well as any other relevant information. You must also record your research carefully.
1. Think about yourself. Choose some media content you like and try to describe why you like this content. Think about your needs, wants and preferences and how to describe your demographic.
2. Look at the listings for television channels for a particular day. Identify what appeals to particular audiences. Pick something that would not appeal to you and watch it, identifying why it appeals to the audience that it is aimed at.
3. Create a spider diagram to present your ideas about one of these texts.

 ONLINE TEST

Head to www.brightredbooks.net to test yourself on researching audiences.

PRODUCTION
INSTITUTION RESEARCH

DON'T FORGET

Keep all your notes to show evidence of your research. You should also keep track of where you get your information from. This will all be helpful to you when you come to explain how your research impacts on your planning.

HOW TO RESEARCH INSTITUTION

When researching institution, there are two main areas you could cover. In analysis, you will have looked at internal and external controls. You can also examine the differing roles of production personnel depending on the role you wish to primarily occupy.

INTERNAL CONTROLS

There are many different controls that could apply to you depending on your brief. However, the most common are budget, time, permissions and available equipment.

Your budget is the amount of money you have available for your production. It is unlikely that this will be very extensive. In fact, quite often, there is no budget. You must decide how you will cope with this and show how this will affect your plans.

Time is often a constraint that massively impacts on production. For example, television programmes often have seven or eight days to complete their production before moving on to the next episodes. Feature films have very strict shooting schedules, including back-up plans if the weather or light isn't right for what needs to be filmed. All productions must stick to deadlines. You will need to consider carefully what your deadlines are and how this will impact on your plans.

Your school or college will have certain rules you should follow. This may include asking permission to film, rules surrounding people being filmed as well as more general codes of behaviour. You should decide how this will affect your plans as well.

The equipment available to you will also vary depending on your school or college. Consider carefully how this will affect your ideas. It may mean you may not be able to include certain effects as a result of the available editing software, for example. Therefore, you must describe what you have chosen to do instead or how you have adapted your ideas to suit available equipment.

EXTERNAL CONTROLS

Depending on the type of text you are developing there will be certain rules and regulations that have an impact on your product. These include health and safety legislation, **copyright** law, certification and codes of practice.

contd

The Health and Safety Executive (HSE) are responsible for ensuring the safety of employees at work. Their advice covers all sorts of industries, including printing and broadcasting. You should find out what rules there are associated with the particular type of product you are making and record how this will affect your plans and ideas.

One of the most complicated areas of research is copyright. If you are stuck, try checking with your local librarian as they will have lots of special training in this area. Briefly, intellectual property such as images and music belong to the copyright holder and you cannot use them without either permission or by paying to use them. This will obviously affect your product and you must discuss how you will accommodate this legislation.

Another interesting external control to explore is certification. In the UK, the British Board of Film Classification (BBFC) are responsible for awarding every film, television programme and music video a certificate to help guide audience members and, particularly, those of a more sensitive disposition to a decision about the suitability of particular content. Video game certification is carried out by the Video Standards Council (VSC) in England and Wales but affects games sold in Scotland as well. Both of these organisations have very detailed websites with lots of information.

There are also specific rules in place for particular forms. One important example is the Code of Advertising Practice, which has separate codes for print and broadcast advertising. On their website, they also have guidance about how these codes work in practice with examples. The Advertising Standards Agency, the organisation responsible for enforcing the code, has judgements on recent complaints as well as information and reports on their website.

ONLINE

Go to our Digital Zone at www.brightredbooks.net/subjects for more links to helpful websites for institutional research.

PRODUCTION PERSONNEL

Another area to investigate is the roles and responsibilities of production personnel. Have a look at information from the careers service to find out what kind of tasks these jobs often include. They will also give ideas about the type of personal qualities needed to fulfil that role that might help you decide whether you would be suited for it.

Production personnel also have to follow certain rules. For example, a journalist, whether print or broadcast, must obey the National Union of Journalists code of conduct. This includes important ideas such as being accurate, fair and honest and the right of the public to be informed. Equity is another organisation that governs careers in the arts and entertainment industry. They include details about the rates of payment for performers.

ONLINE

Go to our Digital Zone at www.brightredbooks.net/subjects for more links to possible sources of information for production roles.

 ## THINGS TO DO AND THINK ABOUT

Just as with Audience, Institution will impact hugely on your intended product. You must record your research and carefully consider how this will affect your content.

1. Look for a film you have watched recently on the BBFC site. What certificate has it been given? Why has it been given this certificate? Were there any changes needed in order to keep it to a particular certificate?
2. Look at the Advertising Standards Agency Broadcast Code of Practice. What rules are in place for advertising to children? Is there anything that cannot be advertised to children?

PRODUCTION
CONTENT RESEARCH

DON'T FORGET
Keep all your analysis notes as well. These will be helpful when you come to plan and also when you evaluate your planning and research.

WHAT IS CONTENT RESEARCH?

Content research is where you use the knowledge you have built up during your analysis unit and apply it independently to help you learn from other texts that are similar to your intended product and to come up with ideas.

CATEGORIES

The key areas to look at here are form, genre, style and tone. With these, you can pinpoint what type of text has been made. Identifying features that help you understand what type of text it is can also help you come up with ideas of what to include to ensure your product fits into that type of text. Purpose is also useful as it helps you consider the purpose of your text.

LANGUAGE

Analysing language is probably the most straightforward part of your analysis and, it is hoped, something you feel comfortable with. Remember to pay attention not just to one particular code but to a range of them. You should also consider how they work together to make meaning.

Technical Codes
Camera angles
Camera movement
Lighting
Soundtrack
Graphics

Cultural Codes
Mise en scène
Colour
Sound – music
Editing

REPRESENTATION

Representation is likely to be a key part of appealing to your target audience. One interesting way to look at representation is to think about what hasn't been shown. Remember everything on screen is very carefully selected so who or what isn't in the product? For example, a Visit Scotland advert would probably include views of hills and lochs as well as people looking happy. It is unlikely to show sad people or the inside of a supermarket. This should help you to work out why what has been included is there.

NARRATIVE

One of the elements of exploring narrative codes and conventions is to think about why they have been used. Does the narrative follow a predictable pattern, meeting the expectations of the audience and providing a satisfying amount of **closure**? Or does the pattern challenge what the audience would expect? Why has this been done? For shock? For humour? To comment on stereotypical expectations?

INSTITUTION

This requires you to think beyond the text itself. What constraints did the text have on it? Were there any problems that came up in production and how were they resolved?

AUDIENCE

Who is the text aimed at and how do you know? This seems quite straightforward but remember you can go deeper than this. Does it meet the needs of the particular audience? Is there more than one audience being targeted? And what about different readings from the audience? Who would not accept the text?

Example:

Calvin Klein released an advert for a perfume called Euphoria ten years after it was first produced. The advert is rather racy and features a model and actress called Natalia Vodianova. She is shot in black and white on a bed and then in vivid, over-saturated colour on a beach. She is wearing a vivid purple dress that swirls around her as she engages in rolling around, sometimes alone and sometimes with a man. The advert uses close-ups of her face to highlight her enjoyment of what is happening and long shots to demonstrate the beautiful setting and the dress. The editing is quick in order to not linger on anything that might cause offence and also to build to a climax. The song in the background urges the woman to 'Open Up like a Wildflower' and the whole advert ends with the tagline 'Free the Fantasy', explicitly linking the perfume to desire and appeal.

On the surface, the advert appears to appeal to women as they are the people who would wear the perfume but really the advert seems more aimed at heterosexual men due to the inclusion of a beautiful woman. The suggestion seems to be that buying this perfume will turn whoever they give it to into a beautiful model and transport them to an exotic beach. Some people probably reject this meaning and say that the advert offers an unrealistic depiction of women as unfeasibly thin and only having worth as an object of desire. Institutionally, Calvin Klein do not just produce perfume but fashion as well. The purple dress is one of their designs and this allows it to be advertised as well. The people who 'photographed' the advertising campaign are also known as fashion photographers who work with Calvin Klein the company, an additional advertisement. As well as internal constraints, the advert also has to avoid suggesting overtly that buying the perfume will make the wearer more desirable and also not show anything too explicit as this would contravene the Code of Advertising Practice as set by the Advertising Standards Agency.

DON'T FORGET

Use the Analysis section of this book in order to help remind you what these terms mean.

VIDEO LINK

Go to our Digital Zone at www.brightredbooks.net/subjects to watch the advert.

THINGS TO DO AND THINK ABOUT

Knowing your competition is a key part of research. This is where content research comes in useful. Knowing what other people do is helpful.

1. Look for a text that is similar to the text you are intending to make that you like and one that you dislike. Use your knowledge of the key aspects to analyse the texts in detail. This will give you some ideas of how they work.

2. Find a text that is aimed at your target audience. Using your key aspects, work out how the text appeals to your target audience. What specific codes or conventions are used?

PRODUCTION
PLANNING

DON'T FORGET

Your planning forms a key part of your assessment. The more coherent and well thought out your planning, the easier it will be to create your product and pass outcomes and the exam.

TECHNIQUES

There are many different ways to plan your media content. By now you will have a clear idea from your brief of what the product you will produce will roughly look like and your research will inform the further development needed. One important concept that you must ensure you hang on to is that you are going to need to justify your decisions and explain why you made the choices you have. This should also be influenced by the research you have completed, and you should be prepared to link your decisions to your research.

MIND MAP

This is one way to start laying out your ideas. Think about the different categories you might need and use those as branches. For example, if you were producing a moving image advertising, you may wish to have a section on images, a section on sound and a section on product. You may even break it into key aspects, examining language, categories, representation and so on.

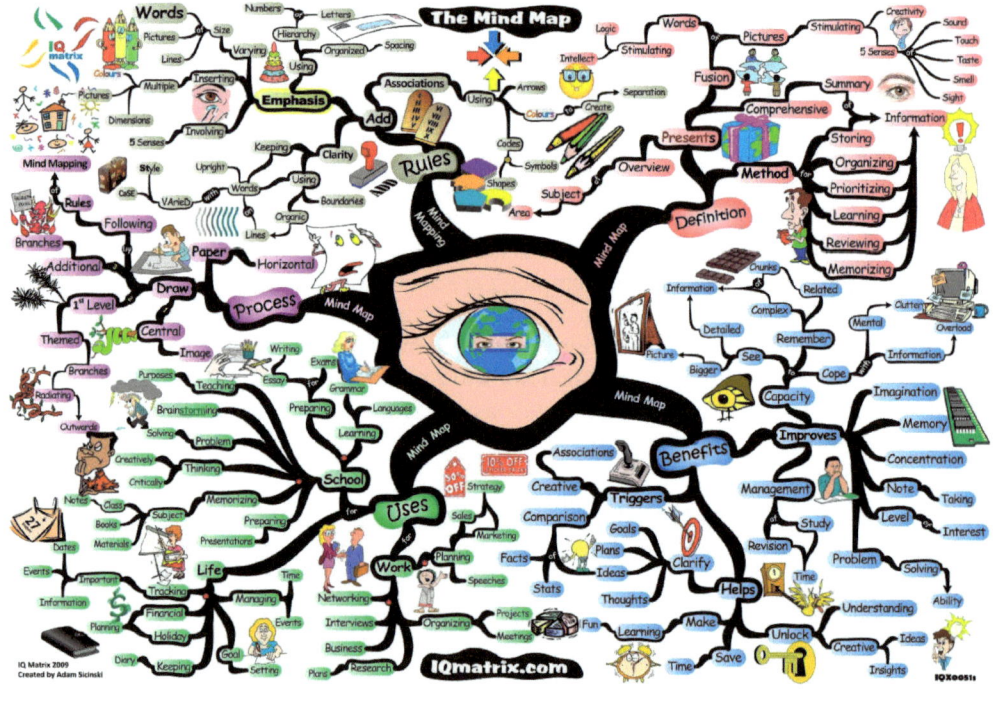

DEVELOPMENT BOARD

If you have studied art, you may be familiar with this idea. You place your sketched-out ideas in the middle of a large sheet of card and annotate it. This would be particularly suitable should your product be a poster or a leaflet. You may wish to use more than one board if you have a number of different sections or a series of texts.

SCRIPTING

One way of planning a product is to script it. This obviously works best for a radio-based product or a moving-image one. Most feature films and scripted television programmes begin with a script or a screenplay. There are software programmes available that help you **format** your screenplay in a professional manner but there are some easy rules to follow that will make your script clear.

contd

Production: Planning

Professional screenplays are typed in Courier 12pt, single spaced as one page equals one minute of screen time.

To open a scene, you need a scene heading, which should be in capital letters and contains a quick one-line description of the location and the time of day.

When you are describing what happens in a scene, it is known as Action. This is always written in the present tense. This includes any sounds or particular set elements that are essential.

When introducing a character, the character's name should be capitalised within the action.

Dialogue is indented and centred on the page with the character name in capital letters above it.

Transitions such as cuts and dissolves should be indicated. Again, these are in capital letters.

Finally, you might want to include specific details on what kind of shot you intend if you are creating a moving-image product. This will give you a clear idea when you come to shoot and will also allow you to discuss language in more depth. Once more, these should be in capital letters.

A professional screenplay for sale (or spec script) will often not include a lot of detail of transitions, shot types or specific set elements as these decisions lie in the hand of the director, producer and set designer. However, you may wish to incorporate some of these to help give a clear idea of your intentions.

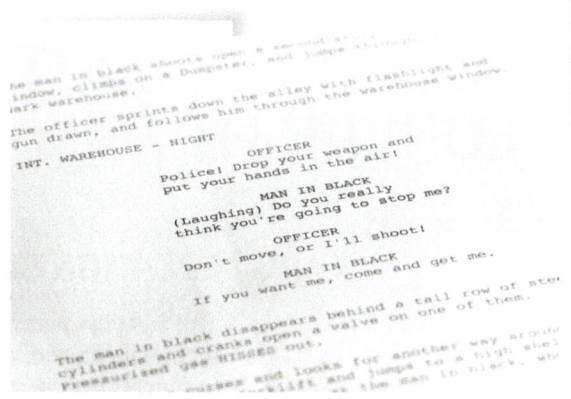

SHOT LIST

Another way to have a more detailed plan like a script or screenplay is to create a shot list. This breaks down each scene into shots and allows you to plan what kind of impact you intend each shot to have. This also means you can include details of the type of sound you intend to include.

STORYBOARDING

Professional moving-image product makers rely on storyboarding to demonstrate their plans and ideas. Your first step is to break your idea into small steps or shots. You should then figure out what you want each of these shots to include. Each shot then becomes a storyboard panel, which is essentially a box that contains an illustration of the shot. You should make notes beside the panel about what is being shown and any audio you intend to include. You can also make note of any transition. This will allow you get a visual feel for the product you are creating.

When creating storyboards, you do not need to have a high standard of artwork. You are using these tools to help you plan out your ideas and compose your product. Stick figures and rough backgrounds are absolutely fine as long as you can make out what you are intending to shoot. Remember, you will not replicate these exactly.

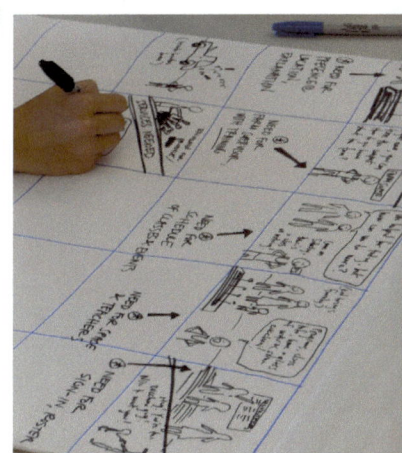

THINGS TO DO AND THINK ABOUT

Have a look at some professional examples of screenplays and storyboards. Search online to find these.

Think about what type of plan will suit you and your product. You may wish to try out a few before you find one that suits you.

Ensure you keep all your planning notes. You will need to refer to them when you are writing up your answers for assessment. You may also choose to create a portfolio of evidence for your assessor or even include references to your plans in your write up and justification.

ONLINE

Go to our Digital Zone at www.brightredbooks.net/subjects for more links to investigate this topic!

PRODUCTION

LOCATION SCOUTING, TECHNOLOGY AND COPYRIGHT

LOCATION SCOUTING

This is a vital part of pre-production and may also be known as the **recce** or reconnaissance of a potential location. This is where you look for specific sites in which to film and get permission to film there. During professional shoots, whether moving image or photographic, the location department works as part of a team. They will follow instructions given by the production team and then present a range of possible options. Some location departments build up a database of potential sites.

Location scouts are not just interested in what the location looks like but also how expensive it would be to film there. Considerations include how far away the location is, whether there are facilities for the crew and cast, the available light and the electrical power available or the need for generators. Permission is also a massive issue as even a small production will cause a lot of disruption.

You must seek permission for filming or taking pictures. Some institutions will have strict rules about filming on the premises and you need to find out about these constraints as well. There might be restrictions on filming people in the background as well. If you are filming outside, you need to take account of the weather and health and safety as well as permission for filming.

A place where a lot of professional filming takes place is Hawaii. In fact, there have been films made there since 1913. It brings so much money into the islands that the government of Hawaii runs an organisation to support film making. They also offer tax incentives to encourage film makers to choose to film there. Weather is one of the major advantages of filming in Hawaii as it has mainly settled, sunny weather all year round as well as never becoming too hot or too cold. The government has also invested in studio facilities and maintains a list of production personnel offering everything from animal wranglers to **VFX** supervisors.

Kualoa Ranch – film location of Jurassic Park in Oahu, Hawaii.

In Scotland, there is a push for the government to form something similar. Creative Scotland has responsibility for promoting filming locations and have built up a database. Permanent soundstages have been constructed in order to provide indoor spaces when Scotland's weather limits filming opportunities. Already the opportunities for filming in Scotland are being seen by the producers of *Outlander*, a British–American production for the US **cable network**, Starz.

ONLINE

Go to our Digital Zone at www.brightredbooks.net/subjects for more links to investigate this topic!

contd

Production: Location scouting, technology and copyright

Blackness Castle, which is used in the *Outlander* series.

TECHNOLOGY

Another important area to research is the technology available to you. Centres have a varied amount of resources and you need to negotiate the use of what you need. You are also likely to come across tools you have never used. This is why time management is very important. You will need to allow time for learning to use equipment, whether it is hardware such as cameras and tripods or software such as computer editing programs.

You will also be responsible for working out what you need. One tool you can use to help you work out how to use the technology you have available to you is the Internet. Often websites offer manuals and tutorials for the specific tools you can use. More general guides might also provide some hints and tips about how to achieve specific effects and create a more effective finished product.

ONLINE

Go to our Digital Zone at www.brightredbooks.net/subjects for more links to investigate this topic!

COPYRIGHT

One of the areas of external constraints that you will need to investigate is copyright law. You will be expected to obey this constraint. This means you cannot use without permission anything that falls under copyright. This could be music, a film clip, an image or a logo. You cannot copy, broadcast or adapt a work without permission. Equally, gaining permission to use a particular image or piece of music may incur a huge cost.

There are ways to avoid breaking the law. You could create your own music and images. You could also find copyright-free images and music online. Some music and images producers allow use under something called Creative Commons, which is a type of sharing that allows some use. There may still be rules you need to follow such as crediting the creator in some way. This is something else you must consider when selecting non-copyright material. Some creators may even designate their work as public domain, which means you can use it without constraint.

THINGS TO DO AND THINK ABOUT

During your **location scouting**, try to take pictures that mimic some of the shots you have in mind. This will help you to identify whether the location is suitable as well as identifying if there is anything you need to move or change.

Make a list of the resources you have available to you. This will provide you with some ideas about the content you could create.

Find a copyright-free piece of music and an image that you could use. What restrictions have the creators put on it?

PRODUCTION ROLES

RECORDING PRODUCTION

THE IMPORTANCE OF SCHEDULES

In the professional media world, film makers often have a very strict schedule to keep to as well as meeting budget constraints and ensuring they gather enough shots and footage to make their production. Equally, other producers of other media must meet schedules and budget constraints as well. By carefully planning out what needs to happen when, it becomes easier to stick to schedules and meet deadlines. However, often unexpected problems crop up, whether the weather is not right for a particular piece of filming or even a member of the team suffers from an illness. Coping with these difficulties and still being able to make good progress is an important part of being a media producer.

You have completed your planning, have a clear idea of what you must complete in order to create your product and have clear deadlines to meet in order to achieve your award. You are ready to set off on your production. However, you must continue to record and document your progress as you work through your creation. In order to ensure you gather evidence of the role(s) you play in making your product, it is essential to keep track of what you do, from meetings with others and research to the actual production and post-production as well. It will also help you remember what you have done and ensure you know what else you need to do. Finally, it will help you complete your evaluation as you will be able to draw on specific examples of challenges you have overcome and be able to discuss these in the required detail.

There are a number of different ways to keep track of your production. You will need to ensure you take time to make notes no matter which approach you adopt.

PRODUCTION MEETINGS

One important way of keeping track of your production is to take notes during production meetings. You will probably be accustomed to taking notes during group discussions and this is very similar. Notes during meetings are known as minutes. It may seem ridiculous to write down what was discussed and agreed but actually taking notes helps to focus your ideas and ensure ownership is taken of decisions and actions. It also helps to keep people who were absent up to date and is a valuable tool to refer back to during your evaluation.

Example:

Production Meeting
Date: 26 October
Present: Greg, Lisa, Evie and Craig

Discussed costume of main character. School uniform was decided to be too stereotypical and boring and it was decided that character would wear ordinary clothing. Decided on T-shirt and jeans. Remembered that copyright means no logos, so we decided to go for a plain black T-shirt. It also helps suggest that character could represent everyone as dressed in a relatable style – not particularly fashionable or identified with any logos or sports teams.

Lisa said she would be able to provide costume from her wardrobe.

The production could be set in many different places. Discussed using the woods around the school as this would provide an interesting backdrop. But as filming will be in December, the weather would probably be bad. Decided to find parts of the school building that did not look entirely like school but could be any public space.

Craig and Greg have decided to do location scouting ...

ONLINE

Go to our Digital Zone at www.brightredbooks.net/subjects for more links to investigate this topic!

PRODUCTION DIARIES

Another way to keep track of what happens during your production is to maintain some kind of production diary. Professional film producers use these to create either behind-the-scenes features or additional promotional material which are often distributed online to build up interest in the film.

Production roles: Recording production

THINGS TO CONSIDER

Paper-based diaries

Keeping a logbook like a diary and writing in it after each session of production is a useful way of keeping track of your production. It does not need to be just a list of activities. You can stick in photographs and note any difficulties or challenges you overcame as well as planning out what needs to happen next. The big advantage of this is that it is easy to carry around and quick to update.

Example:

Production log

Date	Completed	Reflection	Next time
12/9	Completed filming in canteen, transferred to external storage	Changed some long shots to medium shots to focus more on character	Edit scene
14/9	Edited canteen scene, identified shots to reshoot	When editing, realised I had broken **180° line**. Also distracting wall display in background and lighting not great	Reshoot scenes and edit
19/9	Reshot scenes in canteen, edited footage together	Rough scene now complete. Noted changes to storyboard	Move on to stairway scene

Electronic/Online tools

A private social network page, blog or Glow site can be a great place to store your ideas. It is also easy to keep links to images and other useful sites in a useful and easily accessible format. However, you must take care to ensure you check privacy settings to ensure no one you don't want can access your information.

A video blog might be another way to record your production diary. Use an easily accessible camera, such as your smartphone, and discuss what happened during production. This has the possibility of being a really quick and easy way to record your ideas. However, you must ensure you make them available to your assessor.

 **DON'T FORGET**

Be organised! If paper based, use a folder or ring binder to keep similar information together. Electronically, tag your files so you can easily find what you need. This will all help when you are putting together your evaluation.

WHAT TO RECORD

Depending on what medium your production is in, your production log may look different to others in your class. Equally, you may find it useful to use a different structure for different stages of the process. It will need to include details of:

Ideas that are rejected and why
Ideas that are selected for further development
Problems encountered and their possible solutions
Ideas that were successfully achieved
Plans that were changed and why
Self-evaluation of your progress
Further development ideas

THINGS TO DO AND THINK ABOUT

Get into the habit of setting aside time every production session to make your notes and keep your production log up to date. The sooner after doing the work you record what happened, the easier it will be to remember. You can always expand or add to it later if you need to. Don't leave it too long!

Do not throw anything away. You will note down ideas on scrap paper and create spider diagrams to work out some plans. You will take photographs and capture pieces of evaluation when you least expect it. Make sure you keep everything safe.

Experiment with different ways of recording to find what you are most comfortable with. It won't take you long to find out what works best and is most convenient for you.

PRODUCTION ROLES
THE DIRECTOR

THE ROLE OF THE DIRECTOR

The role of the director is a very important role in media production. The director tends to be in charge of creative decisions and the artistic and dramatic choices as well as leading the team of professionals who make a film. Some directors are considered to have a signature style and an overall vision and have become stars in their own right. One theory to describe this is called the **auteur** theory. The director is involved at every stage of production from planning to post-production.

Directors need to maintain a clear idea of what they intend the final product to look like. They must demonstrate good communication skills to be able to communicate this to all other members of their team. They must also be able to make decisions swiftly and confidently.

As a director, you must take responsibility for the product as a whole. While you will be under constraints from your assessor that you must take account of, you will have artistic control of your product in order to allow your ideas and creativity to flourish.

DIRECTOR CLOSE-UP

One of the most famous directors working in Hollywood today is Steven Spielberg. He works in many different genres but is probably best known for his science-fiction and adventure films and for his historical epics. He is also often said to have started the summer **blockbuster** trend with *Jaws*. This film suffered from many problems during filming, especially with special effects. The mechanical shark often did not work particularly well. Spielberg decided to use music and point-of-view camera work to suggest the presence of the shark instead of relying on the prop shark.

Spielberg began making films with a small camera in his back garden using his friends as actors. He then moved into directing television programmes and films before moving to feature films. Spielberg's trademarks include **zooming** in on a character as they witness something terrifying to build tension, using a mirror or a window to reflect a character and interesting background lighting. Spielberg's films often feature music by John Williams, the composer, as well.

MAKING A SHORT FILM

One potential production idea is to make a short film. As ever, the first thing to do is to have a look at some short films. You will see they have a fairly limited narrative with few characters and settings. This is because of a limited budget and a limited amount of time both to produce and in length. In many ways, this mimics the constraints you face, making it an interesting project to approach. It may even make sense to consider making a scene from a film in order to demonstrate your knowledge and understanding of production.

Planning is very important here. You will need to ensure that your idea is manageable and meets the requirements of assessment as well as allowing you to demonstrate a range of skills and roles. Once you have a firm plan, aim to stick to it as much as possible. However, you will find that you will need to adapt your ideas as the reality of filming progresses. You may also come across other ideas or even happy accidents might occur that will give you opportunity to take your product in a slightly different direction.

Example:

Examples of 'happy accidents':

In *Cabaret* (dir. Bob Fosse, 1972), during the 'Tomorrow Belongs to Me' scene in the restaurant garden, a dog runs up the middle of the shot, away from the singers. It can be read as indicating disgust of the natural world at the unthinking acceptance of Nazi ideology. However, it was a stray dog who accidentally ran through the scene and the director chose to keep it in. This scene is also fascinating to look at from the perspective of camera and sound use, for example, the tilt, close-up of characters and changing tempo of song.

During the filming of the opening scene of *The Godfather* (dir. Francis Ford Coppola, 1972), Marlon Brando, playing Vito Corleone, picked up a stray kitten and played with it. This action was unscripted but adds a complex layer to what should be a straightforward terrifying thug of a character.

MAKING A TRAILER

The advantage of choosing to make a trailer is that you have a very fixed form that also allows you to be as inventive and as creative as you want. Watching and breaking down a lot of different trailers will give you a clear idea of what the important elements are as well as providing lots of inspiration.

One key element of trailer making is the length of the trailer. There are different types of trailers – teaser, where excitement is built; international trailers that may promote a particular actor or director over others; cinema trailers that tend to be about three minutes; television trailers that tend to be a minute to a minute and a half and so on. These trailers all have different lengths depending on where they are going to be shown. This is the first decision to make.

The second main decision to make is the genre of the film you wish to advertise. While the film itself may combine genres, the trailer tends to focus more specifically on clearly defined genres to sell itself to particular audiences. This will impact on choice of shots, editing, music, fonts and even the order in which you choose to place shots.

 THINGS TO DO AND THINK ABOUT

Do not let the camera run on. Be disciplined with your shooting. Use two or three takes.

Do not spend endless amounts of time on one scene.

Make sure you transfer your footage to external storage or the cloud to back it up. Having to reshoot because footage is lost will be very frustrating.

Name your files so you can find them easily during editing.

When making a trailer, try to capture a few different angles of scenes so you have more choices in editing. As you have a very short time to make a lot of impact, focus only on important elements in order to convey your ideas clearly.

PRODUCTION ROLES

THE CAMERA OPERATOR

THE ROLE OF THE CAMERA EDITOR

The camera operator is the one who sees all the different elements of lighting and mise en scène work together to create a shot and is responsible for preparing and operating all the camera equipment. On small and amateur productions, they are normally instructed by the director and must communicate with all the different people involved in the filming from the actors to the art department to ensure that these instructions are carried out. On shoots with more budget, a director of photography or cinematographer might also be involved. They are in charge of all camera and lighting crew and are responsible for both technical decisions and artistic choices. They will also be involved with post-production image manipulation as well.

Camera operators often have to consider where to position the camera. In some cases, where the technology is available, they will also be able to select different lenses and supporting equipment. They have to be creative and able to solve problems as well as confident enough to offer suggestions to the director to help improve the content. They need to listen carefully as well to help capture what is required.

SOUND EDITOR

The sound editor has a very important role in creating the sound in a production. They are responsible for bringing together the dialogue, any effects and music to make the text effective. In big-budget features, for example, there may even be separate editors for each element. In addition, sound may be added through the uses of **foley**, which aims to recreate ambient sounds and take out anything unwanted, often drawing from an established sound library. The Wilhelm Scream, for example, has been used in more than 350 films and is now a bit of an in-joke.

| ONLINE

Go to our Digital Zone at www.brightredbooks.net/subjects for more links to investigate this topic!

CAMERA OPERATOR CLOSE-UP

Can you name a camera operator? Probably not. Camera operators tend not to be very well known as they are often responsible for carrying out instructions.

John de Borman was born in France in 1954 but is recognised for working on some of the biggest British films of all time such as *The Full Monty* and *Made in Dagenham*. He is also a director of photography and has worked on productions all over the world, from the US to Nigeria. In addition to working on feature films, de Borman has also worked on television programmes and advertisements. He has worked for major brands such as Gucci, H&M, Guinness and BT.

De Borman originally trained as a sculptor before teaching himself how to operate a camera. He started by working on music videos and adverts before moving into the world of feature films and major television drama. He has won many awards for his skills, including the Lumiere Award for his contribution to British cinema from the Royal Society of Photography in 2013.

MAKING A MOVING-IMAGE ADVERT

Moving-image adverts are probably the first thing that you think of when you hear the word advertisement. Adverts are a very familiar form and people have strong opinions about their favourite adverts.

Adverts follow a lot of rules, both from a legal perspective and from an internal institutional perspective. There are strict limits on timing and rules about what adverts cannot show or promise. They require a lot of research in order to ensure that these restrictions are kept to.

Length is a major component of advertising. Advertising space tends to be sold in time blocks of 30 seconds, which means that adverts tend to be 30 seconds, a minute, a minute and 30 seconds or two minutes long. Moving-image adverts can have extended versions that tend to be shown in cinemas or distributed online. Sometimes adverts can last for an entire break in a programme (for example, Ronseal) but these still only last about three minutes.

There are also different types of adverts for different purposes. The most common is probably selling a product but there can also be adverts that promote a message. These are adverts that inform the audience about issues such as road safety or healthy eating. These are known as Public Service Advertisements or PSAs.

THINGS TO DO AND THINK ABOUT

Camera movement can be an issue. Think about how to move the camera in order to keep it smooth. Using a camera that is designed for movement might be an idea or thinking about how to keep movement smooth on wheels rather than walking might help. Using technology such as a drone may also help you maintain a smooth movement.

Always remember to think about whether the camera or the operator will be captured in the shot. This is important if working with more than one camera.

Sound is a tricky part of filming, especially for amateurs. Are you going to use a microphone? Can you record a voice-over? If outside, there is often wind noise (even on calm days) and if indoors, there can be echo. Think carefully about where you are filming for effective sound.

Try out different angles and movements to offer options. Be guided by the storyboard and plans but try to be creative as well.

PRODUCTION ROLES
THE EDITOR

THE ROLE OF THE EDITOR

There are a number of different types of editing depending on what type of text you are creating. Generally, editors select and prepare written, visual, audio or moving-image content. Editors are often seen as the organiser and the selector as well as the corrector.

PRINT EDITORS

In publishing, there are a number of different editorial roles. The editor-in-chief tends to be the person in charge of producing the publication. They delegate tasks to their staff such as reporting, developing articles and advertising, motivate and manage staff before finally checking everyone's work as the publication goes to print. Newspaper editors can have a great deal of power over opinions as they can select which stories to include and which ones not to. Often different sections within the publication have lead editors as well, such as business, sport, fashion and so on. News organisations often organise editors like this, who have responsibility for content throughout the organisation, whether it is online, in print, on the radio or on the television.

Sub-editors tend to be responsible for checking the written text before publishing. They check that it is spelled correctly, uses good grammar and that it fits the style of the publication. In some cases, sub-editors also write headlines and edit articles to fit the available space. This is important when working in print because there is a finite amount of space. Sub-editors will also check facts and copyright and **crop** photographs.

ONLINE
Go to our Digital Zone at www.brightredbooks.net/subjects for more links to investigate this topic!

MOVING-IMAGE EDITORS

Moving-image editors may also manage staff on large productions. They are one of the key department heads under the director and are responsible for putting the moving-image content together in a way that best conveys the ideas of the director. Often, the editor will be attached to the production from the very beginning, looking over the screenplay, and will also be working on the text long after any filming has been completed, right up until music and sound has been finalised.

Moving-image editors have to select the best takes and craft them together to create scenes. They need to have a sense of the entire text to cope with any filming that happens out of sequence. Editors nowadays are also technology experts, dealing with a range of editing software. In the past, editing was often literally done by cutting the film and sticking it to the next piece. Luckily, computers have made the process much easier to play with variations and undo mistakes if necessary.

CLOSE-UP ON THE EDITOR

Print

Anna Wintour is probably best known as the inspiration behind *The Devil Wears Prada*. She has been editor-in-chief of *Vogue*, the prestigious fashion magazine, since 1988. She initially worked in fashion before moving into publishing. She built a reputation for interesting magazine spreads and for discovering models and designers. When she was hired as *Vogue*'s editor, the magazine was becoming less relevant. Wintour reorganised the staff and focused on more modern consumers.

Wintour began making more media appearances in 2009 and became something of a celebrity with her trademark bob and large sunglasses. She uses her fame to promote the magazine and the company she works for and has had a documentary, *The September Issue*, made about her time at *Vogue*.

contd

Production roles: The editor

Moving image

Margaret Booth (1898–2002) worked as an editor in the very early days of film, editing work by D. W. Griffith. She followed Louis B. Mayer to MGM when it formed in 1924 and worked there for more than 40 years. When Booth was editing, she famously said she preferred directors to stay out of the cutting room entirely. She is also credited with popularising the invisible editing style or **continuity editing** that dominates cinema nowadays.

While she was Oscar-nominated (for *Mutiny on the Bounty* in 1935), it was not until 1977 that she received an honorary Oscar for her services to the film industry as an editor.

MAKING A NEWSPAPER OR MAGAZINE

There are a number of computer programs that are available to help you with laying out magazine and newspaper pages. Knowing what you have available to you will help you plan out what you want to do. There are a number of elements of a newspaper and magazine page that have technical terms that will help you work out how to organise your content as well.

Key terms

Masthead/Title piece – the newspaper's title displayed on the front page.

Headline – a phrase that summarises the main point of the article. Headlines are in large print and different style in order to catch the attention of the reader.

Byline – the line above the story, which gives the author's name and sometimes their job and location (known as the dateline).

Photograph/Graphic – helps make the page look more interesting; it can add understanding of a story and/or entice someone to read the article.

Sidebar – this is a panel or box on a page containing graphics or other information about an article. It is eye-catching and breaks the story up into different elements.

Crosshead – bolded/large text that breaks up a long story.

Pull quote – a quote from the story that is enlarged and appears within the text.

Standalone picture – a story that can exist on its own or on a front page leading to a story inside.

It is likely that the newspaper or magazine you produce will focus on issues local to your establishment. You must make sure you check carefully that you are allowed to use images. There may also be child-protection issues surrounding the use of names of young people. There will be a local policy in place. This can form another part of your research.

MAKING A DOCUMENTARY

An increasingly popular style of film is the documentary. Some people say this is because documentary makers such as Michael Moore (*Bowling for Columbine* and *Farenheit 9/11*) and Morgan Spurlock (*Super Size Me*) are such controversial figures, attracting press attention. There are others who believe it is increasingly popular due to the widening distribution channels streaming and cable companies have provided, notably Netflix and HBO. There are different types of documentary: expository, which speak directly to the viewer, often using voice-over and have a strong point of view; observational, which aim to record reality without comment or re-enactments; interactive, where the documentary maker participates in the situations in the film; reflexive, which draw attention to the fact they are constructed and make the viewer consider the 'reality' of what is recorded; and performative, which aim to explore emotions and personal experience.

The secret to making a successful documentary is to start with a focused question. It is not enough to pick a topic you are interested in. The topic should be something you are passionate about, however, as your enthusiasm will drive the production. It doesn't have to be serious and worthy. A documentary is still a film and still aims to entertain an audience as well as being informative or even argumentative. Remember to use all the film language tools at your disposal.

 ONLINE

Go to our Digital Zone at www.brightredbooks.net/subjects for more links to investigate this topic!

 THINGS TO DO AND THINK ABOUT

Research is very important to non-fiction texts. You must check your facts – a good rule is a minimum of two sources. You should also use reliable sources and watch out for bias and prejudice.

PRODUCTION ROLES

THE PRODUCER

THE ROLE OF THE PRODUCER

In the world of film, television and advertising, the producer is an interesting role to take on. Essentially, a producer's role is to oversee the entire production, from raising funding and hiring staff, including the director, to seeing the project finished. A producer may even be involved in distribution and promoting the film. A producer must have immense troubleshooting and organisation skills as they will be responsible for setting the production schedule and ensuring the content comes in on budget. They are the leaders of the creative team as well, ensuring each department works together.

The producer is often the first person involved in a project, identifying a script or even acquiring the rights to a book or story. They may be office based, organising filming from a distance or they may need to be on set in order to troubleshoot. Producers often have a team to lead directly to aid them with their production responsibilities as well as motivating and coordinating the wider production. This may include accountants and secretaries as well as assistants or runners who do whatever is required.

TYPES OF PRODUCER

Executive producer – an executive producer is a credit often given to the major funders of a film. They do not tend to be involved in the film creatively but will demand a profit. In television production, this role changes as an executive producer can often be the 'showrunner' or person in charge of the entire production, taking a role in writing and hiring directors who will change as the series progresses.

Co-executive producer – this tends to be a studio executive or a distributor who has provided funding to the film as well.

Co-producer – works under the producer and helps with the cast, the finance and the post-production.

Line producer – mainly in charge of the budget.

Associate producer – a reward for doing their job particularly well, whether on set or behind the scenes in funding.

ONLINE

Go to our Digital Zone at www.brightredbooks.net/subjects for more links to investigate this topic!

CLOSE-UP ON THE PRODUCER

Jerry Bruckheimer works in both film and television. He tends to work in the fields of action, drama and science fiction. Among his credits are *CSI: Crime Scene Investigation*, *Top Gun* and *Pirates of the Caribbean*. He started by working in advertising but has now moved on to huge Hollywood blockbusters. While his films are not often considered particularly favourably by critics, he is immensely commercially successful. Promotion for his products often use his name as he is one of a few producers who have a high public profile.

MAKING A POSTER

Posters are one of the most common types of advertising you are likely to see. They advertise everything from local events to huge commercial billboards.

When thinking about creating a poster, there are many things you need to consider. One of the most important is layout. In the Western world, people tend to read left to right, top to bottom and posters follow this pattern, with the top left tending to have something to grab attention and the key information at the bottom. There is often a strong single image that has been chosen to appeal to a particular audience. For example, in film poster advertising,

contd

the image will often be of a central 'star' if they have been cast in that film. If the film is based on an iconic character, a symbol to represent them will often be very visible.

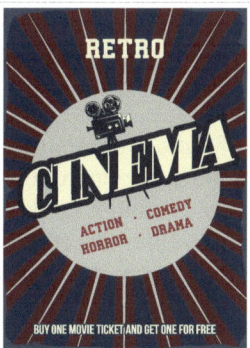  
 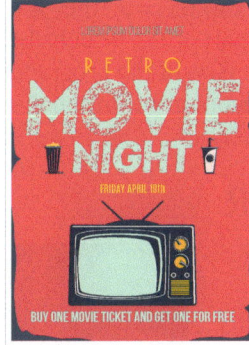 

Text is also important to consider on a poster. Too little and the meaning of your poster will be unclear, too much and no one will be able to read it. Posters tend to be passed by very quickly and include only key information – more of a tease to entice the audience. Font is also very important. It is essential it is clear and readable. The wrong font can make a poster seem badly designed. Imagine a poster for a serious science-fiction film. Now imagine it in Comic Sans.

Posters can often be used for public service information. Posters aimed at health and safety are often placed around young people promoting ideas such as safe driving, healthy eating and mobile phone use. These might be helpful to you as potential topics to investigate.

MAKING A PRINT ADVERT

Print adverts follow many of the same rules regarding posters – strong images, good choice of font and text. However, print adverts offer the opportunity to include more information. This can be in the form of text or in the form of images.

Print adverts are basically advertisements printed on paper. This can be within another publication, such as a magazine or newspaper, or it could be a flyer, a leaflet, a direct mail advertisement or essentially anything that is both printed and portable. Magazine companies and newspapers make a great deal of their income from print adverts and often produce packs to promote their product to advertisers known as press packs, which include rate cards or lists of how much different print adverts will cost.

THINGS TO DO AND THINK ABOUT

Remember to consider where everything works on the page. There are a number of strategies for analysing posters and print adverts – use them to help you organise your own ideas.

There should be a reason for everything on the poster or print advert. Remember to justify why the elements have been included. If you cannot justify it, should it be there?

PRODUCTION ROLES

RADIO

THE RADIO PRODUCER

The radio producer has a managing role in the production of radio programmes. This can be from coming up with ideas or choosing ideas from others, carrying out research and bringing in presenters, guests and other content all the way through to using the technology available to actually record the broadcast. They may offer direction to presenters and performers as well as responding to any listener comments or complaints. The producer tends not to be heard by the listener.

Radio producers are often involved with running the business of radio production, such as managing budgets and resources. In this way, they are similar to a film and television producer. Health and safety is also part of the responsibilities of a radio producer as well. The producer provides an objective view of the programme and can give suggestions about improvements as well as reassuring the presenters that the programme is going well.

THE RADIO PRESENTER

A radio presenter is responsible for being the 'voice' of a radio show. They are the ones who present the ideas, build a relationship with their listeners and keep the show going. Having very strong presentation and performance skills is obviously important but the ability to work under pressure, stay calm and think on your feet is also essential. Presenters also have to be competent with a range of technology in the radio studio as well. Presenters also help establish the style and tone of their programme.

ONLINE

Go to our Digital Zone at www.brightredbooks.net/subjects for more links to investigate this topic!

Radio presenters often write their own material. They must have good communication skills in order to clearly express ideas. Interviews are an important part of the radio presenter role as often they must speak to the individuals involved in whatever is being explored, whether they are politicians or musicians or whether they are people with a story to tell. Therefore, being able to research and design questions is also an important part of a radio presenter's role.

CLOSE-UP ON THE RADIO PRESENTER

Stuart Maconie started as a journalist and musician before moving into radio producing. His interest is in music and he became a music reporter on Radio 1. He also presented a show about albums. He later worked across the BBC, presenting documentaries and standing in for other presenters. As his focus is music, he took a major role in working with BBC 6 Music, focusing on diversity in music, particularly being concerned with more alternative genres. He has since used his radio fame to move into writing books and appearing on television in programmes about music.

MAKING A RADIO PROGRAMME

One of the key elements of a radio programme is going to be the content you include. The next most important thing will be the presenter you choose. Voice is the most important thing here. A voice that is warm, pleasing, clear and interesting is going to be more successful than someone who is unclear and flat. Personality that translates will also be important.

With content, it is important that your understanding of the topic is excellent. You need to know all the different sides. If you are interviewing a guest, you should research them thoroughly to be able to ask interesting questions. You should also make sure you prepare your questions as you do not want to be caught without something to say. Try to avoid lots of jargon and statistics and think about what the listener would be most interested in hearing about. Sticking rigidly to a script is also not necessary – being able to pursue something interesting and being able to think on your feet are also important skills.

MAKING A PODCAST

Podcasting is an audio programme designed to be distributed through the Internet. In many ways, it is like a radio programme in that the presenter's voice and personality is often what drives the success of the show. However, as a podcast is distributed online, it does not have to obey the strict rules of time and broadcast rules that radio must stick to. Equally, often podcasts might be considered 'narrowcasting' as they tend to focus specifically on a very specific topic. This means they tend to have a narrower but more loyal audience.

ONLINE
Go to our Digital Zone at www.brightredbooks.net/subjects for more links to investigate this topic!

There are people who say that editing too much can be bad for podcasting as it disrupts the flow of something that is often quite natural. Equally, talking over one another makes listening very challenging for the audience – in real life or with visual input, it is easy to work out who is talking. This becomes very challenging when only listening. One strategy is to record onto different tracks rather than recording onto the same track. This allows you to take space out speaking, take out strange noises and coughs or splutters as well as misspeaking.

THINGS TO DO AND THINK ABOUT

One of the major issues of recording a radio programme or a podcast will be scheduling. If you intend to include a guest, you must take into consideration when you will be able to record them as well as recording everything else your programme requires.

Technical considerations such as bad volume and poor audio quality play a major part in the success of anything audio where this will be much more distracting than in visual form. Unwanted noises like headphone feedback, mouth noises and background noise also have to be taken into consideration. Microphone technique is also something you should research, and you should aim to use a pop filter. Rather than a rigid script, show notes that guide you will often help you to stay on track and avoid filling in space with time wasting.

PRODUCTION ROLES

THE WEB DESIGNER

THE ROLE OF THE WEB DESIGNER

Web designers have a number of responsibilities that are both technical and non-technical. They are responsible for planning and coming up with ideas, creating and then coding webpages. Often, they have to work with clients who have specific requirements as well. Therefore, communication skills as well as technical skills are essential.

With the proliferation of different platforms and devices as well as different access needs, checking and testing is a major part of any web designer's job. Quite often, they also take responsibility for providing technical support or training the client's team in how to maintain and update the website. Research is also needed to ensure the content is correct and up to date as well as complying with the law and other rules and requirements. There are often design trends and developments that should be taken into consideration as well.

ONLINE

Go to our Digital Zone at www.brightredbooks.net/subjects for more links to investigate this topic!

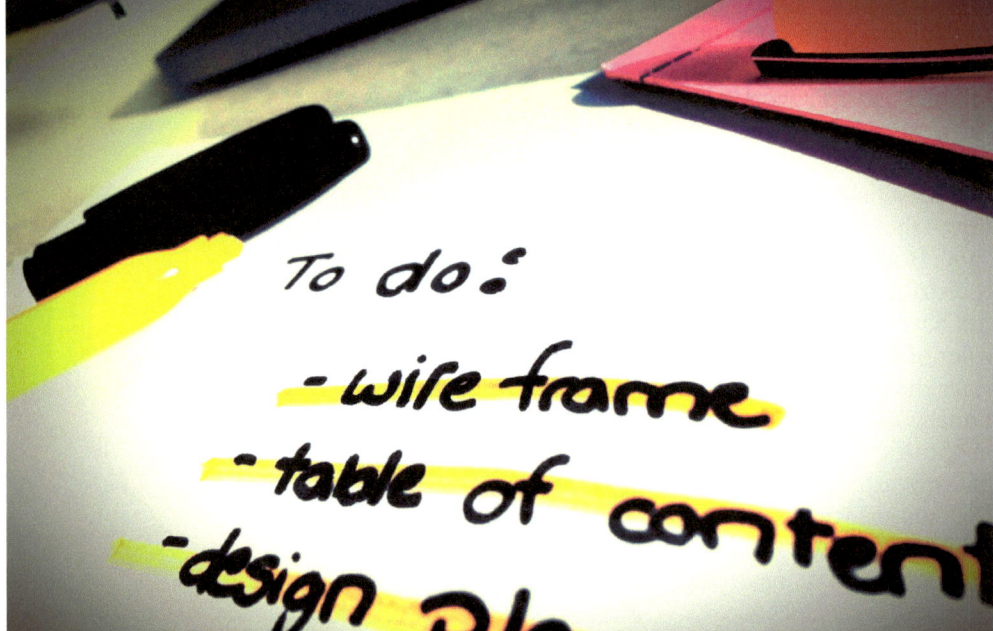

CLOSE-UP ON THE WEB PAGE DESIGNER

Ethan Marcotte is an American web designer best known for coming up with the idea of responsive web design. This idea came out of the flexibility of web pages and the proliferation of devices and suggests that web design should break away from the restrictive structure of print and towards something that was more adaptable to the user. He suggests that designs need to take account of the devices that may visit the site rather than developing separate device-specific sites. He also recognises that accessibility can be varied across the world, particularly connection speed. He says, 'My goal is, irrespective of technique, to make the web as accessible as possible and as beautiful as possible for the people who are trying to access it.'

Marcotte has created websites for *People* magazine, The Sundance Film Festival, *The Boston Globe* and the School of Visual Arts, among others. He is also a frequent speaker at web design conferences across the world, including Adobe MAX, An Event Apart, and Webstock.

MAKING A WEBSITE

One of the first steps when making a website is to research what similar websites have done. Finding out what works for you and what doesn't is an important part of coming up with ideas. Online, people have short attention spans and grabbing and keeping that, as well as making it clear where to go and find information, is absolutely essential. Using clear navigation and standard terms for finding things such as contact details should be a priority. Ensuring that you provide all the relevant information is also important to ensure that the visitor finds everything they need.

There are many different types of software available to help with web design and finding out what you have available to you will be an important research task. Images are very important when designing a website, both graphics and the photos that provide real detail. But equally important is the language you use. Ensure it is as accurate as possible – nothing makes a website look untrustworthy more than spelling and grammar mistakes. Similarly, including too much jargon or sounding too formal is equally off-putting. Having a clear, straightforward idea of what you want to put across is essential to developing a successful website.

MAKING A VIDEO GAME

Another possible production idea may be to develop a video game. Video game designers need to plan, design and create the game, although they often work as part of a team. Video game designers can be focused on art, but they also will need to know computer programming. Understanding how games function is also an essential part of designing a video game. Video games can roughly be split into two main areas to consider – the mechanics and the content. The mechanics are the rules that the computer game uses to actually play the game. The content includes the environment, the storyline and the characters.

Genre is often an essential part of considering game design. In video games, genre is quite different from film or television genre. Some suggested genres could be abstract games, educational, strategy games or sports. Research into these as well as the influence rating systems have on games will be essential to developing a full understanding of the industry as well. An important part of making a video game will be to test and ensure there are no bugs in the video game.

THINGS TO DO AND THINK ABOUT

Embedding means putting video, audio and pictures into the text of a website. This is what makes a website so different from print. Think about how to balance all these exciting elements with loading speed and also clarity.

Search engine optimisation is a really important part of successful websites. Use key words in web headlines, standfirsts and captions to make sure the site comes up as high as possible on a web search. A key word needs to be used as near to the beginning as possible so that your audience knows they are on the right type of site.

THE ASSESSMENT

EVALUATION

THE IMPORTANCE OF REFLECTION

Looking back at your experience and reflecting on it is an essential part of production. This can include thinking about your personal strengths and weaknesses in production, the finished text and also thinking about what you could do next time to improve your product.

One way to begin your evaluation is to ask yourself these three questions:

What went well?
What didn't go well?
What would I change next time?

Even though these are very general, they will start you thinking about what you are proud of and help you identify ways in which you could improve. Once you have these, you need to add more detail, refer to specific examples and use suitable media terminology.

THE BRIEF

Looking back at your brief is another good way to consider your evaluation. You will have agreed some decisions to do with content, form and audience with your assessor and assessing whether they were the right decisions to meet your brief is also something to consider and explain.

You can also look back at your initial creative ideas and see how effective your research and planning has been in achieving your aim. Often in evaluation students focus heavily on the final product but thinking back to how you began the project may help you gain some valuable insights.

PRODUCTION LOG

Now is also the time to use your production log to think about skills such as time management, completion of tasks and fulfilment of roles. Your production log, whether on paper or electronic, is a very useful tool to help you remember what you did and when you did it. It can also act as a reminder of all the work you have completed. As production can take place over a period of weeks or months, this is very helpful and helps you complete your evaluation fully.

KEY ASPECTS

A useful tool is to go back to the key aspects and analyse your product as you would professionally produced media content. You will have practiced this throughout the course. Refer to the Analysis section of this book to help remind you as well.

Categories – does your text fulfil its purpose? Does it fit into a particular genre?
Representation – how have you depicted people, places, events and ideas?
Narrative – which narrative codes and conventions can be applied to your text?
Language – how has your use of language combined to create meaning?
Institution – how have you dealt with constraints, both internal and external?
Audience – how does your text appeal to your audience?

This will help you *justify* your decisions and your choices. This justification is essential to your evaluation. Why you have chosen to do something specific rather than something else and why you haven't used something you had planned to might also be a useful way of approaching your evaluation.

PEER-EVALUATION

Another way to begin your evaluation is to work together with other people in your class and ask them to help you judge your product. This is known as peer assessment and you will be familiar with this from other subjects. This is useful as other people offer a fresh perspective and will often be able to see the positive side of your text whereas you will perhaps focus more on the parts that didn't quite work.

PRESENTING YOUR EVALUATION

There are a number of ways to present your evaluation and your assessor will help you decide what is right for you. Here are some suggestions to help.

Essay

This is probably the most common way of presenting your evaluation. Essay writing is a skill you will have developed in the years you have been in education. Remember, however, that this is an evaluation and you may prefer to use headings and extended bullet points and include images rather than just paragraphs. You may also wish to include examples of your planning by referring to your storyboards or to your production by including your production log.

Presentation

For those of you who prefer talking to writing, a presentation can often be a very effective way of presenting your evaluation. As your product will have a visual component of some kind, this allows you to point to specific examples and explain your ideas in detail. It is essential that you are prepared fully as your assessor may ask you questions, and you will need to speak in a great deal of depth.

Mind map

Using graphic organisers is often an excellent way to see the links between different ideas and concepts. Mind maps are one of the most commonly used in schools. There are even software programs to help you develop your mind map. The advantage of these is that it never runs out of space unlike paper. Using different colours, images and highlighting will also help you to explain your ideas fully.

Remember to allow time to fill in your production log as you complete each section. This will make your evaluation easier as you will be able to refer back to it as you think about your product and your performance.

THINGS TO DO AND THINK ABOUT

As you progress through your production, you may make decisions that you wish to justify. Make notes in your log or record these ideas in some way. This enables you to complete parts of your evaluation as you produce your product.

Remember to use the media terminology you are learning about to describe your product.

Discuss your ideas with your assessor. They will have kept track of your progress as well and will be able to offer some suggestions. However, you are responsible for your own record keeping. The more evidence you have gathered, the easier it will be to evaluate yourself and your product.

THE ASSESSMENT

UNIT ASSESSMENT

CREATING MEDIA CONTENT

Creating Media Content (Higher) unit is an optional part of the media course. The idea behind this unit is to give you an opportunity to develop the skills needed to create media content and to evaluate your progress. It is also expected that you will be able to acquire another perspective on the key aspects and build your skills in using media terminology.

Your assessor may examine the unit as a separate unit from the Analysing Media Content (Higher) unit or choose to combine assessment of the two units. You will be expected to analyse your creation using your developing analysis skills, so this does give you the opportunity to overtake a range of outcomes in that unit as well. You may undertake these standards by creating a single product or your assessor may choose to have you undertake a range of tasks to build up evidence.

NATURALLY OCCURRING EVIDENCE

One of the terms you may hear when undertaking this unit is naturally occurring evidence. As you work through the unit, your assessor will observe you and may keep a checklist or notes as you show evidence of overtaking some of the unit outcomes. You should also keep all your notes and documentation as this will help your assessor to see your progress and achievements.

PLANNING AND RESEARCH

In order to overtake this standard, you have to work closely with your assessor to negotiate at least two areas of the brief. This could be what the content will be about, which genre it will fall into, what form or medium is most appropriate, who the audience should be and what purpose your product is aiming to meet. Your assessor will also make sure you are aware of the resources you have available to you to help with your production. This should help you to develop your ideas. You are then ready to plan and research your product.

Research

Before you begin researching, you should try to work out what you need to find out. A KWL grid might be helpful to you to work out what you know, what you want to know and then to record what you have learned. You may identify key words to help you search as well. Looking at professionally produced content will be an important part of your research whatever your brief is as you are aiming to emulate that.

Planning and developing Ideas

One of the things you should aim to do is think about a number of different ideas. When working professionally, media producers often have to show a range of potential ideas to their client and this helps prepare you for that. You should plan and research more than one idea in order to think about a variety of options. These plans need to be detailed, which means they should not just say what you hope to include but should explain how you will create meaning by referring to a range of technical and cultural codes and conventions. This means you do not just explain what is being used but why you are using it and what the intended meaning is. You may find it helpful to link these to your research.

DON'T FORGET

Remember, you are not just carrying out research in isolation. You are aiming to draw some conclusions that will help you make decisions when planning your product.

PRODUCTION

The key word behind production at Higher is *sustained*. This means you should fulfil your production roles fully and over a period of time. You will also be expected to carry out at least two roles. Your roles may be technical or non-technical and you may be working independently or as part of a group. Regardless, you should aim to show that you understand the responsibilities of not just your roles but the wider roles and responsibilities your chosen medium demands.

It is not just knowledge of roles you need to demonstrate. You also need to show understanding of a range of media codes and conventions to help you create finished content that meets the brief. You must produce a finished product that clearly shows your contribution. This is important if you work as part of a group. One way to make sure you record the roles you take on and to demonstrate your contribution is to record your progress in your production log. Manage your time efficiently in order to do this as clear records will help prove your achievement of the assessment standard.

EVALUATION

To overtake this standard, you must make at least four points with detailed reasons about the effectiveness of your performance over the whole production process. You can discuss:

Planning
Research
Your production roles
The product
Ways in which you can improve next time

Detailed reasons should include a clear reason for focusing on that particular point as well as references to your performance, the plans and research, working as a group or using technology. You can draw on anything that is relevant as long as you explain fully why it is important. This might link to the brief, your intentions or the context in which you have made your product. You might draw upon references to professional production work or even compare your product with other content. You might even find it helpful to refer back to the key aspects.

EVIDENCE

Your evidence for passing this outcome will tend to be generated over a range of time and is likely to include your notes, your product, your production log and conversations with your assessor. It is essential that you keep all your notes. You will be guided throughout the process by your assessor as well.

THINGS TO DO AND THINK ABOUT

Don't just jump on the first idea you come up with – you need to develop a few ideas so take your time and complete your research for each fully before moving on to the actual production process.

Build up a portfolio of evidence. Keep all your notes. If you hold meetings with your group, take minutes like a professional organisation would. Don't discard storyboards once you have completed a scene.

Experiment with ways to keep track of your production. A vlog or blog might suit you as readily as writing lots of notes. You can evaluate as you go along as well – as long as you keep the evidence.

THE ASSESSMENT

THE ASSIGNMENT — PLANNING

OVERVIEW OF ASSIGNMENT

The assignment is worth 50% of your final mark. You will complete the assignment within your centre and then it is sent to the SQA for marking. It aims to assess your ability to apply the knowledge and skills you have developed throughout the course and should be completed independently. You may have help from other people with permission from your assessor if you need them for technical reasons.

The assignment must be your own work, although you will receive reasonable support from your teacher or lecturer. You will have to take into consideration a range of possibilities when planning and solve problems that are likely to show up during production. Equally, you will draw on the knowledge of media techniques, terminology and the key aspects that you have built up while working through both units. The assignment also lets you reflect on the experience of creating your product as well as the challenges you have faced and worked through.

There are two sections to the assignment. Planning is worth 30 marks and so is development. You must ensure your product is complete before you submit it otherwise you will not meet the requirements of the assignment.

> **DON'T FORGET**
> Time management is key. You must meet deadlines to ensure you complete your assignment to the best of your ability.

PLANNING

Section 1 is divided into six sections each worth five marks. You gain these marks by discussing your plans for your product and justifying your planning decisions by making reference to your research.

Your assessor will provide you with a rich brief offering lots of choices for you to make regarding your interests, your desired target audience and even your purpose.

Your write up is sent off to the SQA for marking. There are up to 30 marks available for discussion relating to:

Creative intentions in response to the brief (5 marks)
Content research 1 (refer to at least one key aspect) (5 marks)
Content research 2 (refer to at least one different key aspect) (5 marks)
Production role(s) (5 marks)
Audience research (5 marks)
Institutional context research (5 marks)

You will gain one mark for each relevant, developed point you make, so you should try to make five separate points for each of the areas and should use headings to structure your work.

There are no official guidelines for length, but you are expected to provide detailed and complex justification. In the region of 500 words per section will give you a rough guide to the amount of detail needed. Just saying what your decisions were or saying what you found out in your research will not get you any marks. You need to explain why you made choices and link your ideas to your research findings. If you refer to something like your storyboards, you may want to include them as well, but it is not required.

> **DON'T FORGET**
> Remember – you can include your storyboards, scripts and notes if you want to make reference to them.

ANSWER EXAMPLES

When completing your write up, it is a good idea to plan out your answers first. Remember it falls into two sections and you might find it easier to write up your planning before you move on to the actual production.

Imagine your brief is something like 'Produce an advert to promote an in-school activity to a group of pupils.'

contd

The Assessment: The Assignment – Planning

You might start by discussing what your initial ideas about your product were. This is why keeping all notes is very important.

Example: Creative intentions

The brief suggested to me that I would need to produce either a poster or a moving-image advert. A poster could be displayed around the school whereas a moving-image advert could be shown at assembly. The poster would continually remind pupils of the event whereas a moving-image advert might attract a more captive audience but only once.

I decided that in order to reach as many pupils as I could, a moving-image advert would probably provide a better impact than posters that might be read and might be ignored. This is because I asked pupils where they tended to get information about school events from and 73% said assembly made more of an impact than posters around the school. I also decided I would investigate the possibility of putting the advert on the school website or having it played on the flat screens that are in the canteen. Because it would be a little bit unusual, this would hopefully mean more people would see it more than once.

I decided that the school activity I would advertise would be the sponsored walk for charity. This felt like a good event as people haven't been supporting it as much, as I found out that participation has dropped from 90 per cent to 60 per cent and it is very important. It would also help people to know what to expect, especially in S1 where they would not have done the walk before …

DON'T FORGET

Remember – you can include your storyboards, scripts and notes if you want to make reference to them.

Each section of your write up is worth up to five marks. You are aiming to make five detailed points per section. Have a look at the exemplar answers for audience research:

Example: Audience research

As my audience was school pupils, I decided to do some research to find out what people already knew and what they wanted to know about the sponsored walk. I decided to run a small questionnaire with a selected group of pupils from each year group. I approached their PSE teachers and asked if I could have them fill it out during PSE. Their teachers thought that this would be a good plan. I have attached a copy of my questionnaire and my results analysis.

My results suggested that people thought the sponsored walk was 'boring' and 'pointless'. They also seemed to want to know 'where does the money go'. A significant percentage also wanted to ask, 'Why can't I just give money rather than have to walk?' There was no difference between genders about who preferred the walk or didn't. Younger year groups were much more inclined to take part than older years.

I decided that this would mean I would have to produce an advert that contained information about where the money had gone in the past. I spoke to members of staff on the charity committee and they were able to show me photographs and letters from nominated charities. I then got in touch with the charities to ask if I could use these images. I received permission, which meant I could incorporate them in my product.

I also received permission to use photographs from previous sponsored walks that showed people smiling and laughing. There were even some video clips. By using these, I thought it might suggest to the audience that the walk wasn't boring and was lots of fun. I also decided to tackle the importance of doing exercise for benefiting physical and mental health by researching some statistics. I looked at the NHS website (www.nhs.uk/livewell/fitness/Pages/Fitnesshome.aspx), which gave me lots of information. Since it was from a reliable source, I thought people would respect it. I emailed the NHS Choices website and received permission to incorporate these as well.

I also thought that parents might be a secondary audience as they would be interested in finding out what the sponsored walk was about and also what their children might need to bring and wear. I decided to include a short section that outlined equipment, such as suitable shoes and comfortable clothes, as well as highlighting the importance of bringing water and a packed lunch or money to make purchases at the halfway point.

DON'T FORGET

Points must specifically link to your assigned brief and your plans.

Here the candidate makes a number of points about their research, explaining different areas they needed to find out about. It also explains where they found information, what the information was and what decision they made as a result. Linking your research and your decisions is an important part of justifying your decisions.

THINGS TO DO AND THINK ABOUT

Try to come up with five different areas to discuss under each of the question headings. Refer back to your notes and add in specific details about what you needed to find out, where you found information, what you found out and what your planning decision was as a result.

THE ASSESSMENT

THE ASSIGNMENT — DEVELOPMENT

CONTENT AND EVALUATION

The development section contains two sections, making your content and evaluation. Again, this should provide you with the chance to put into practice skills you have developed over the course.

Step one is to create your media product using the different skills you have acquired. Once you have done that, you then have to write up your evaluation of the whole production process. This is known as the development. This is then judged alongside your actual product so it is very important to ensure you take as much care as you can in producing your product and meeting all deadlines.

There are 30 marks available for this section and the marker will consider your content and your evaluation together. Your content should be the best that you can make but as the course is not focused on artistic or technical skills, these are not taken into consideration. Therefore, the justification is really where you gain marks.

Your content needs to be sent to the SQA along with your justification. If you have to put your product onto another medium, such as a USB stick, check it has transferred properly.

Your justification breaks into two sections:

a Evaluate the production process and evaluate how effectively you carried out your production role(s) within the institutional context.

Give at least four developed points of evaluation. You should refer to the final content and/or elements of the development process to support your evaluation. If you worked within a group or class project, you can refer to the whole content and/or process, or your individual part(s). (10 marks)

b Evaluate how effectively you used media codes and/or techniques to achieve your creative intentions in the finished content.

Give at least five developed points of evaluation. You should explain how you have used media codes and/or techniques and evaluate how effectively you have done this. You must refer to particular examples from your finished content to support your evaluation. (20 marks)

Again, there are no official word limits but in the region of 1000 words for **a** and 2000 for **b** gives you a rough idea of the depth you need.

In Section **a** you could talk about how the external key aspects of audience, institution or society fit your product, or you might talk about your fulfilment of a particular production role. You could also write about institutional factors such as external and internal controls, health and safety, budget and resources or anything appropriate.

Section **b** needs to link your points to specific examples. You could write about the technical and cultural codes you have used to convey your meaning, target your audience or achieve your purpose. It is not enough to discuss one single code, for example, a particular camera angle. You should include reference to a range of codes, such as a combination of camera work and editing, which convey meaning. You could also discuss an element that runs throughout the content, such as tone, representation or even narrative structure.

DON'T FORGET

Your product forms part of your development. The actual quality of the content will obviously depend on the resources available to you, so this is not part of what is assessed. Instead, the assessor is focused on your creativity and your ability to work well and overcome problems.

ANSWER EXAMPLES

Evaluate the production process and evaluate how effectively you carried out your production role(s) within the institutional context.

To achieve lots of marks here, you should aim to explore at least four points and develop these in detail. You must ensure you point to specific and detailed

contd

examples from either your product or the process in marking your product to back up your ideas. Linking these to either the way institutions work or the problems that arise from internal or external constraints is essential to demonstrate you understand how these have affected your product. The definition of what to include is quite extensive so use your notes to expand on your ideas.

Example:

Music was something I struggled to find and incorporate in my advert. I originally planned to use a piece of copyright-free music but finding something suitable was quite challenging. I tried a few websites that promised to provide copyright-free music but quickly discovered that the types of music I wished to include that were quite upbeat and poppy were often in a foreign language and I thought this would be quite distracting for my audience. I knew I had to obey copyright law as an external constraint and as my budget was zero, I would not be able to pay a composer or artist for a familiar piece. In the end, I contacted another pupil at the school who plays in a band and they agreed to let me use a piece that they had written and performed that fitted my advert well. I did have to agree to put an acknowledgement of who had created the piece of music in order to help promote their band, which seemed like an acceptable compromise. In fact, I have seen some adverts and television programmes starting to do this to advertise the music being played as well. In the end, it made the music a much bigger part of the advert, which I was able to use to further appeal to a wide audience as there was interest from pupils who also liked the band.

This candidate starts by outlining a problem they had to overcome. They linked the issue to their planning and then explained what decision they made and how it affected their text. It is also interesting how they then go on to link this to the audience impact of the advert.

Evaluate how effectively you used media codes and/or techniques to achieve your creative intentions in the finished content.

For marks to be gained here, you should aim to make at least five developed points. The assessor is looking for you to comment on the use of media codes and techniques that you then need to link to your intended meaning, audience or purpose. You need to back this up with specific examples. It is also not enough to describe one single code and its connotations at Higher. You are aiming to look at either a part of your product that uses a range of codes that combine to create meaning or you might refer to something that runs throughout the entire product.

Example:

The representation of my main character, The Girl, was very important throughout the text and I used a number of codes and techniques to create this. The most obvious was costume. I chose to have The Girl in her school uniform at the start but as she became more and more involved with drug taking, I chose to have The Girl lose elements such as her tie, which signifies being very smart and instead adopt more and more of a slovenly look. I also used make-up here to help my actress. She starts the advert with quite a healthy look, but I was able to use paler make-up and draw dark circles under her eyes to convey the idea that everything was going wrong. Hair was also an important element. To create the idea that The Girl wasn't looking after herself, I used water to create the idea her hair was lank and greasy. This all added up to create the visual impression of negative changes happening to the character. This linked to my purpose, which was to promote an anti-drug message, as it showed that the main character was becoming more and more ill and unhealthy.

Here the candidate has chosen to focus on representation of their main character throughout their product and discussed their use of elements of mise en scène, namely costume, hair and make-up. They then go on to explain what impact this had on the text as a whole, linking it to purpose.

 THINGS TO DO AND THINK ABOUT

Is there something in your product that you think is particularly effective? Perhaps it is a short sequence or something that helps your entire product. These are the sorts of elements you want to highlight in media codes and techniques. Use your new vocabulary of key aspects and technical terms here.

GLOSSARY

180 degree line/rule – the moving-image 'rule' of having an invisible line crossing the set in order to maintain narrative continuity.

Academy Awards – also known as Oscars. High prestige awards given by Motion Picture Association of America (MPAA).

anchorage – a way of 'tying down meaning'; without anchorage meaning could be polysemic – open to various interpretations. For example, a caption anchors meaning to a photo, and music anchors mood in a film.

archetype – a character type or pattern of action, which recurs, related to universal myths. For example, the hero, the quest.

attitudes – used when discussing audiences. These are the positions people adopt in relation to a particular issue.

auteur – a film director whose films show a personal vision or style.

BAFTA – British Academy of Film and Television Arts. Given in Britain to reward both film and television excellence.

beliefs – used when discussing audience. Beliefs are deeply held views.

best boy – assistant to the chief electrician on a film set.

blockbuster – high-profile films with big budgets and tie-in, spin-off and theme park potential – made by major studios.

brand – a created set of images and ideas associated with a particular name or product.

broadsheet – a large size newspaper such as *The Herald* or *The Guardian*.

cable network – as opposed to a broadcast network (US), subscriber service, considered to be more permissive than traditional networks. Often focused on a narrower audience.

camera angle – used to describe the position of the camera relative to the action.

celebrity – someone who is famous.

CGI – computer-generated imagery. Uses computer graphics to add to the visual world of the film.

classic narrative or classic Hollywood narrative – the dominant narrative mode found in **mainstream** film, which uses traditional narrative structure (equilibrium, disruption, return to equilibrium) and continuity editing to give clarity.

close-up – where the camera is positioned close to the character. Tends to include character's head and shoulders.

closure – the completion of a narrative in a classic narrative, for example, the happy ending in which the hero defeats the villain.

composition – the arrangement of visual elements for clarity or attractiveness within the frame.

connotation – the meaning associated with a sign; for example, a red rose could be associated with love.

constraints – issues that productions must overcome. Could include budget or be more external and include laws and rules.

context – external aspects of a text that shape its style and meaning, for example, the audience, social and institutional contexts.

continuity editing – also known as invisible editing. Aims to hide the constructed nature of the text and flow without drawing attention to itself.

conventions – the expected elements that are included in a particular type of text.

copyright – law covering ownership of content, particularly text, images and sound.

cropping – cutting parts from an image, often used to create preferred reading.

cross-cut – a type of edit where two scenes are spliced together to show that the sequences are occurring simultaneously.

contd

Glossary:

cultural codes – sign systems that are shared by members of a culture, for example, dress, gestures, language.

decoding – the processes by which media audiences interpret meaning in a media text.

demographics – the social characteristics of an audience, for example, social class, age, gender.

denotation – the description of a sign, for example, the dictionary definition.

diegetic sound – the sound that actually comes from inside the scene like dialogue or weather, not added later like music or a voice-over.

direct address – making the audience feel that they are participating in what is happening; for example, newscasters use direct address as if they are speaking directly to the viewer. This can be known as 'breaking the fourth wall'.

discourse – systematic ways of presenting representations so as to express particular ideologies or myths, for example, nationalistic discourses in sports coverage and the discourse of the countryside as natural, peaceful and beautiful.

dolly – see track.

dominant ideology – when the beliefs of the majority or powerful groups in society dominate.

effects – the impact that media content has on the audience.

Emmy – US television awards presented by the Academy of Television Arts & Sciences (ATAS), the National Academy of Television Arts & Sciences (NATAS), and the International Academy of Television Arts and Sciences (IATAS), rewarding excellence in different television areas.

encoding – the process by which media producers construct meanings in a text.

eyeline match – a technique of continuity editing; for example, a shot shows someone looking off screen, and the next shot shows what they are looking at.

fade – a moving-image edit where the screen gradually fades and disappears, leaving a black or white screen.

filter – placed over an image or film to change the look or colour.

flashback – a scene that disrupts the chronological narrative, set in the past or recalling past events.

font – the design/style of characters in the typeface.

format – the recipe for producing a media product in a particular genre, for example, hard news at the beginning, sport at the end of a newspaper or news programme.

genre – a set of conventions or common practices that guide the production, marketing, identification and interpretation of texts.

globalisation – the domination of the world's media by transnational media conglomerates leading to media products aimed at the international market rather than local interests.

Golden Globes – film and television awards presented by the Hollywood Foreign Press Association.

grip – lighting and rigging technician, helps with operating the camera and setting up lighting.

handheld – camera movement that mimics the use of a camcorder or mobile phone. Often quite shaking and disorientating. Helps create sense of immediacy. Associated with news footage.

hegemony – the dominance that powerful social groups and their ideology have in society, to the point that it seems natural.

high angle – camera pointing down from height to make characters look weak and vulnerable.

high key – very bright lighting with few shadows.

hybrid – a cross between two things. Used often to refer to two genres mixed together.

icon – a type of sign that has a close resemblance to what it represents, for example, a photograph or a portrait. Someone idolised by others, for example, pop star or politician.

ideology – set of *attitudes, beliefs* and *values* that are held in common by a group and reinforced by their inclusion in media.

contd

GLOSSARY

indie – short for independent. Means the production is not part of a major studio or label. Often used to mean quirky and original.

intertextuality – links between texts, for example, genre, stars, subject matter, spin-offs.

jump cut – two shots from approximately the same position that are slightly different set next to each other to create excitement or a sense that something is wrong.

jump scare – where an object or character suddenly appears on screen with the purpose of making the audience scared.

juxtaposition – the side-by-side positioning of an article/item in relation to others that gives added or contrasting meaning.

licencing – studios selling rights to images and brands to other producers to create merchandise.

location scouting – looking for a location to shoot a film or a photograph.

low angle – camera pointing up from the ground to make a character look taller and more powerful.

mainstream – popular texts.

market research – research into possible audiences.

master shot – a camera shot used, normally at the beginning of a sequence, to show where everything and everyone is to help the audience make sense of the action.

match on action – a technique of continuity editing. A shot shows someone starting to move and then the next shot shows them finishing the movement – the viewer follows the action and does not notice the cut.

merchandise – products that are based on films, for example, T-shirts, toys and books. The aim is to make more money for the text owner.

mise en scène – whatever happens in the frame, that is, characters, set, props and so forth.

mode of address – how the text speaks to its audience, for example, direct or indirect.

montage – an editing technique combining several shots, which are not necessarily related. A conspicuous technique, unlike continuity editing.

non-diegetic sound – sound that is added over the top of a text, often to anchor meaning. Typically, music or voice-over.

pan – camera moving from side to side in fixed position.

recce – see location scouting.

SFX – special effects within a live action shot. These can include optical effects, such as the use of matte paintings, or more mechanical effects, such as the use of miniatures or pyrotechnics.

shot – a single piece of moving image, often edited with other shots to create a sequence.

star – someone who is famous for being very good at their profession. Often used in music, sports and cinema.

Steadicam – camera mounted on body of camera operator, able to be taken into middle of action.

tilt – camera moving up and down from a fixed position.

track – camera changing position in any direction. Also known as a **dolly** shot.

values – used when describing audience. Values represent the moral or ideological structure within which beliefs and attitudes are formed.

VFX – video effects outside the physical world of the live action. Computer-generated imagery (CGI) is part of VFX.

voice-over – a narrative from a character that has no obvious source. Can be internal monologue or can provide extra information.

zoom – camera movement where the camera either becomes closer (zooms in) or goes further away from (zooms out) a subject.